BRADNER LIBRARY
SCHOOLCRAFT COLLEGE
18600 HAGGERTY ROAD
LIVONIA, MICHIGAN 48152

SCHOOLCRAFT COLLEGE LIBRARY

3 3013 00121336 6

HQ 536 .S7695 2007
Stracher, Cameron.
Dinner with dad

WITHDRAWN

BRADNER LIBRARY
SCHOOLCRAFT COLLEGE
18600 HAGGERTY ROAD
LIVONIA, MICHIGAN

Also by Cameron Stracher

Double Billing
The Laws of Return

Dinner with Dad

How I Found

My Way Back

to the

Family Table

Dinner
with Dad

Cameron Stracher

 RANDOM HOUSE
NEW YORK

HQ
536
.S 7695
2007

Dinner with Dad is a work of nonfiction.
Some names and identifying details have been changed.

Copyright © 2007 by Cameron Stracher

All rights reserved.

Published in the United States by Random House, an imprint of The Random House
Publishing Group, a division of Random House, Inc., New York.

RANDOM HOUSE and colophon are registered trademarks of Random House, Inc.

Grateful acknowledgment is made to Alfred Publishing and BMG Music Publishing
for permission to reprint an excerpt from "Once in a Lifetime," words and music
by David Byrne, Brian Peter Eno, Chris Frantz, Jerry Harrison, and
Tina Weymouth, copyright © 1980 by WB Music Corp., Index Music, Inc.,
and E.G. Music Ltd. All rights on behalf of itself and Index Music, Inc., administered
by WB Music Corp. Copyright © 1980 by BMG Music Publishing Ltd (PRS)/
Warner Tamerlane Publishing Co./Warner Chappell Music Limited.
All rights for the world administered by BMG Music Publishing Ltd (PRS). All rights
for the U.S. on behalf of BMG Music Publishing Ltd (PRS) administered
by Careers-BMG Music Publishing (BMI). Reprinted by permission
of Alfred Publishing and BMG Music Publishing.

ISBN 978-1-4000-6537-0

LIBRARY OF CONGRESS CATALOGING-IN-PUBLICATION DATA
Stracher, Cameron.
Dinner with dad: how I found my way back to the family table/Cameron Stracher.
p. cm.
ISBN 978-1-4000-6537-0
1. Dual-career families—United States.   2. Work and family—United States.
3. Parenting—United States.   I. Title.
HQ536.S7695 2007
306.8720973—dc22   2006035877

Printed in the United States of America on acid-free paper

www.atrandom.com

2 4 6 8 9 7 5 3 1

First Edition

Book design by Mary A. Wirth

For Christine, Simon, and Lulu.

And you may find yourself in a beautiful house,
With a beautiful wife
And you may ask yourself—
Well . . . how did I get here?

—TALKING HEADS, "Once in a Lifetime"

Dinner with Dad

It's 7:37 P.M. Do You Know Where You Are?

I am running for the train at Grand Central when I see him: a man, about six two, thin, shoulders beginning to hunch prematurely, balding, prominent nose and cheekbones. He carries a laptop case slung over one shoulder and a gym bag over the other. His eyes have the weary look of a man who has not yet had dinner but suspects it may be too late. One hand darts nervously to his ear, holding a cell phone or a BlackBerry. The other hand clutches the bag as if it's his last best chance. He looks left, then right, like a skittish cat, as he navigates the crowd loitering at the fast-food stalls, ducks oncoming traffic, and dashes for the train.

I follow him through the platform doors. For a moment I lose him at the bottom of the stairs, then he reappears by the second car. A gray man in a gray suit, chewing nervously on his lip. An apparition. A reflection. A warning.

My doppelgänger.

If he notices our resemblance, he doesn't acknowledge it as he surveys the crowded car from the vestibule, then chooses a seat near the front. He withdraws a soft pretzel from his gym bag, breaks off a piece, and chews slowly and deliberately as he slumps against the window. I continue past him and sit at the other end of the car.

The train is filled with lawyers, bankers, and advertising executives making their evening run up the golden corridor of Metro-North's New Haven line: Greenwich, Stamford, Darien, Westport, Southport, Fairfield. It is a commute with which I have become too familiar in the four years since I left Manhattan. A commute I never thought I would be making. A commute that sucks the soul from me in great gulps and fouls the air like the smell from the backed-up bathrooms and the socks of the hedge fund trader who insists on putting his feet on the vinyl seat.

It is 7:37 P.M. I am late. Again.

My life took a turn for the worse when I stopped making dinner. Not all at once, but gradually, stealthily, until the life I had lived resembled nothing at all of the life I was living. One day I was carefree, creative, happy, and loving; fifteen years later I was impatient, claustrophobic, angry, depressed, and resentful. Once I had been thoughtful, romantic, attentive. Now I ignored my wife and stomped about the house. Once I had dreamed of a certain success, now I dreamed of dreaming. I took pills to help me sleep, and pills to keep me awake, and pills to smooth the transition between the two.

I can see the moment of transition as clearly as if I graphed it. But at the time it's not as if I could have said: "Here, this is where everything will go downhill." If anything, when I moved back to New York I thought my life was beginning its upward trajectory. Little did I know.

I learned to enjoy cooking during my first years out of college.

In a sweltering Somerville apartment I made my first jambalaya in a huge cast-iron skillet. In graduate school in Iowa City, traveling, to the food co-op was one of the highlights of my day. Buying beans in bulk, grinding my own peanut butter, discovering locally roasted coffee was almost too much fun for a single person. Sure enough, I met my wife at the co-op. In a little black dress and a pair of Doc Martens, she was serving cheese and crackers to discriminating shoppers. Our love blossomed as we experimented with making our own *garam masala* and ghee. Warm afternoons spent baking samosas. Black bean burritos, fried wontons, and scrambled tofu. Neither of us was an expert, but we were energetic, and willing to try anything at least once. With each new meal we wooed each other, expanding our repertoire as we broadened our affection. Making food together was almost as much fun as sleeping together, and often led directly to it—the bedroom was right off the kitchen. Dinner was the first step of a dance that would last the rest of our lives. Or so we thought.

Soon, Christine's *Moosewood Cookbook* sat on the shelf next to my *Joy of Cooking*. My *Classic Italian Cooking*. Her *Greens Cookbook.* She was twenty-five, red-haired, blue-eyed, her lips like something to rest on. I was thirty and still fit enough to work out with the Iowa track team. I had postponed a career in law to write the Great American Novel and fallen in love with a poet from Idaho. We spent three years living together on East College Street, reading Marianne Moore and Alan Dugan, Michael Cunningham and Marilynne Robinson. When it was time to leave, we took our spices with us, jars with labels we handwrote: *coriander, cumin, rosemary, thyme.*

At first, New York City seemed the perfect move for a couple whose first date was at the only authentic Mexican restaurant in eastern Iowa. Within a few blocks of our Upper West Side apartment, we were surrounded by culinary representatives from most of Latin America as well as India, China, Vietnam, Thailand, Ethiopia, and the entire European continent. But life would be different in New York, as I quickly learned when the managing partner at my law firm called me in to his office to tell me he had noticed I wasn't working as late as my colleagues. Most of the associates ate dinner together in the firm's small conference room, and I was conspicuously absent. My hours had suffered, as had my work. His warning made me realize I was going to lose my job unless I ate dinner with the other lawyers—whom I barely knew and didn't care for. We weren't in Iowa anymore.

For the next few years I ate from some of New York's best restaurants—in the comfort of a windowless room—as I learned to ply a trade about which I was ambivalent at best. The law was not the intellectual challenge I had expected, but a dull grind through a mountain of paper: tedious, amoral, and merciless. I brought home leftovers for my wife, who had taken to ordering in from Burritoville or Ollie's while she graded English papers. Our tiny kitchen barely held enough food for breakfast, let alone a full meal. When we did eat together—on weekends and vacations—cooking was a distant memory. Instead, we subsisted on white cartons, aluminum containers, and plastic utensils. I rose most mornings at five to continue writing what would become my first novel, while the buses and garbage trucks rumbled below on Broadway.

The birth of our son and then our daughter forced my wife back to the kitchen. But it was a journey she made alone. As it was for many Manhattan parents with small children in a cramped two-bedroom apartment, mealtime was a multistage affair: kids, then adults, then leftovers. Though Christine managed to turn out the occasional dish with tofu or chickpeas, the logistics of preparing a meal for four in a kitchen with two burners, one chair, and no oven rarely flamed the culinary imagination. The living room dou-

bled as a dining room; the sink became a table, and the food pyramid an Egyptian hieroglyphic. Strange smells from other apartments wafted up the hallways, few of them inspiring confidence in
the gastronomic talents of our neighbors, most of whom we
avoided as we clanged up and down the elevator. If New York was
a melting pot, there were some funky things burning.

In the mornings, I walked my son to preschool. In the
evenings I often jogged home alone, detouring through Central
Park for a few extra miles. Professionally, my career had finally
gathered momentum. I was working for CBS, doing First Amendment litigation that I enjoyed, and had published a novel and then
a memoir about my indentured servitude in private practice. By
the time my son started kindergarten, I was writing a third book,
traveling regularly for work, contributing to various publications,
teaching, and practicing law. I was the typical overachiever, unable
to say no to anything, incapable of pulling my hand back as it
reached for the next brass ring, keeping my gaze fixed on the distance, wondering what was just over the horizon.

But no one owns New York; we just rented it. The city was no
place to raise a family, despite the proliferation of strollers on the
sidewalks. Kids needed space, light, grass, and schools that didn't
cost twenty-five thousand dollars and require IQ tests, achievement tests, blood tests. Their parents needed peace. On West
Eighty-sixth Street, my son's first word was "loud." My daughter
played in a sandbox without sand. And so, after eight years in
Manhattan, we bade farewell to our tight quarters, telling ourselves we were headed for a better, more spacious abode, with
room for us and a table for dinner. We went north, as so many had
before us, venturing into southern Connecticut where Mr. Bland-
ings had built his dream house and John Cheever had torn it
down. We would be content with a serviceable kitchen.

With a fifty-five-mile commute, however, getting home in

time to eat, let alone cook, was a practical impossibility. I rarely returned before eight or nine o'clock at night, which was simply too
late for our children. Sometimes my wife waited for me; more
often, I picked up something at Grand Central and ate on the
train: pizza from Two Boots, samosas from Café Spice, a turkey
sandwich from Junior's. Some nights I didn't come home at all. In
addition to teaching at New York Law School, I was working for
a media insurance company in Kansas City, which required frequent trips to the Midwest. The travel to Kansas, along with the
commute to Tribeca, made me feel like a man without domicile,
an itinerant mercenary, a nomad.

I never imagined, when I was stir-frying in my Iowa City
kitchen, that I would become the father who left for work in the
morning before the sun rose and returned after his children were
asleep. As a man who taught his wife to make *risotto ai funghi*, I
assumed I was safe from the dull conformity of suburban life, the
stratified gender roles of *Ozzie and Harriet* and *Leave It to Beaver.*
Yet here I was, trudging to the train station to catch the 6:01, the
newspaper clutched in one hand, a half-eaten bagel in the other.
That was me wandering around the parking lot trying to find my
car in the darkness. One day I stopped cooking dinner, and the
next day I woke up in a gray flannel straitjacket. What was a father
to do?

I leave the train at Green's Farms station. A dozen other men and
one woman exit with me, all of them from the rear car like battle-
hardened veterans who know the exact location of the stairwells
and the shortest distance between two points. My doppelgänger is
nowhere to be found, and I assume he departed at an earlier station, proximity to New York being a direct reflection of the size of
a man's wallet. Westport, where I live, is not exactly the golden

mean, but it is more affordable than Darien or Greenwich, and certainly better than Rye, Scarsdale, or Larchmont, the hallowed Westchester suburbs where the commute is at least thirty minutes shorter and houses are proportionately more expensive.*

By the time I arrive at my home, it is 8:55. My daughter is asleep, but my son is awake, and lies in bed reading Archie comics. He has gone through two boxes of his mother's old comic books, and is now rereading his favorites. His long legs stretch across the blankets, and he wears a dozen "Live Strong" bracelets of various colors on his left wrist and a seashell necklace around his neck. Nine years old, with size nine feet, a mop of sandy brown hair, and as skinny as a broom handle.

"I thought you said you were coming home early," he says.

"I was, but I got stuck on a conference call."

"What's a conference call?"

I wish only for my son that he will never experience a conference call, that the world of corporate machinations will forever remain foreign to him. Lately, he has been IMing me in my law school office. I find it both startling and depressing, like a man who has discovered hairs sprouting from his ears.

I describe my telephone conversation with the insurance claims handler I was counseling, but he has already returned to his comics. I kiss the top of his head and tell him lights out in ten minutes.

Across the hallway his sister is asleep, one arm splayed above her head, the other clutching a stuffed puppy. She wears a pair of

---

* A rough formula might be expressed thus: $H = (Bd + Ba) (100,000) \times (25/M + SAT^2/nSAT^2)$, where H is housing price, Bd is the number of bedrooms in a home, Ba is bathrooms, M is the number of miles from Manhattan, and SAT is the average SAT score at the local public school while nSAT is the national average.

her mother's old pajamas, which are nearly thirty years old but fit her perfectly. Her hair is bleached a summer blond from chlorine and salt, and she wears a rope bracelet around one ankle. I brush a damp lock of hair from her mouth and tuck her gently back into the blankets, then close her door behind me.

I go downstairs and retreat to my office, where I reply to e-mail for the next forty-five minutes. When I emerge, it is nearly ten o'clock, and I startle my wife in the kitchen.

"I thought you were upstairs," she says.

"I was checking my messages."

"I was about to come up."

Instead of responding, I thumb through the mail on the kitchen counter.

"How was teaching?" she asks.

"Okay," I say, ripping open the electric bill.

"Are you coming to bed?"

"In a few minutes."

I'm not exactly sure why I can't put away the bills, or why I have to check my e-mail compulsively, or why I sequester myself in my home office with the door closed. These are things that I should probably talk about, but I can't.

My wife shrugs, and leaves me there in the kitchen. I wish she would try harder to coax me upstairs, but given my unresponsiveness, I can't say I blame her. I have become untouchable in the last few years, immune to expressions of affection, until my wife and children have begun treating me like a cantankerous uncle, tiptoeing around my bad humor and swollen feet.

I finish separating the payment demands from the catalogues and credit card offers. I throw the former on my desk, and the latter in the trash. I remember, as a kid, wishing I could receive as much mail as my own father did; now that I do, I realize all he received were bills.

Finally, I trudge to the bedroom and find my wife asleep with the lights on and a book splayed across her chest. Her glasses have slipped crookedly down the bridge of her nose. As she lies there, the tension drained from her brow, I can see the faces of our children in hers: the broad plane of my son's forehead, my daughter's high cheekbones, his freckles, the swoop of her lips. I lift the glasses from my wife's face and set the book on her nightstand. Then I brush my teeth, swallow an Ambien, and climb into bed beside her.

I do not dream.

The alarm clock wakes me, it seems, before I have slept. Fumbling for my flashlight in the dark, I find my clothes and the suitcase I have packed the night before and stumble downstairs. Too tired even to make coffee, I slather a piece of bread with peanut butter, fold it in half, and wrap it in a napkin to eat in the car. I stick my cell phone in one pocket, my BlackBerry in the other, my Palm in my laptop bag, and my wallet in my jacket. I disarm the alarm, unlock the double locks, and trigger the motion detector on the outdoor lights as I walk to the garage. My car is cold and smells damp, the result of three steady days of rain. As I back down the driveway, I cannot see the stars.

On the Merritt Parkway the cars drum steadily past me despite the fact that I am driving seventy miles an hour. In Idaho, I think, where my wife was born, and where she urges us to move, people go to bed at a reasonable hour and the highways are never jammed. No one drives to the airport at 4:20 A.M.

But this is the road I have chosen. I set the cruise control and listen to the AM radio tell me where I can get my hair transplanted, my back waxed, my forehead lifted, and my teeth whitened. When I cross the Whitestone Bridge I can just make out the skyline of the city, the missing towers reminding me of the day I turned around on this same road and headed back to my new home in the suburbs. I was a younger father then, my daughter barely two years old, my son just starting public school. Boxes from our old life lay scattered about our living room while the television beamed its images of conflagration and destruction. As awful as that day was, I couldn't help but feel we had left Manhattan at just the right time, literally days before, shielding our children from the horrors of the real world the way good parents should.

Now, not for the first time, I wonder why we left the city, what we hoped to find, what we were running from. I wonder, again not for the first time, whether staying would have changed anything. I wonder about choices, roads not taken, sins of omission and failures of imagination. I wonder about the questions I didn't ask, the answers I didn't know, and the reasons I avoided seeking.

At the airport I park my car, walk across the deserted garage, and check in for my flight to Kansas City. At a kiosk I buy *The Wall Street Journal, The New York Times,* a pack of gum, and the largest coffee I can find. I board the plane and sit with my face pressed against the window, the cold air against my cheek like a wake-up call.

When the plane banks left, I look down on the city. Missing something, I think. Missing. Something.

A Man, a Plan, Burritos

We are a nation that eats alone.

Hunched over the sink, jammed behind the wheel, stupefied in front of the television. We take our meals to go, wrapped in a pita, a tortilla, a hot pocket, a bun. Our fridges filled with juice boxes and snack packs, our freezers and pantries with Hungry Man, Lean Cuisine, Annie's, Amy's, and Aunt Jemima. Our favorite appliance is the microwave; our second favorite, the toaster oven. Our kitchens have never been larger or better equipped, yet more likely to be empty and unsullied by food. What we've lost in desire, we've made up in firepower. But no one is cooking.

The decline in the family meal has been well documented, and blamed for everything from the rise in obesity to drug abuse, behavioral problems, promiscuity, poor school performance, illegal file sharing,* and a host of other ills. A recent study at Harvard Medical

---

*During the controversy over the Grokster case, a record-industry spokesperson was quoted as saying that kids were "stealing" music over the Internet because parents no longer sat down to teach them morality over the dinner table.

School, for example, concluded that the odds of being overweight were 15 percent lower among those who ate dinner with their family on "most days" or "every day" compared to those who ate with their family "never" or on "some days." The National Center on Addiction and Substance Abuse at Columbia University found that teens from families who almost never ate dinner together were 72 percent more likely to use illegal drugs, cigarettes, and alcohol, and that those who ate dinner with their parents less than three times a week were four times more likely to smoke cigarettes, three times more likely to smoke marijuana, and twice as likely to drink as those who ate dinner with their parents at least six times a week.

Blame television. Blame Clarence Birdseye. Blame McDonald's, Burger King, KFC. Blame the suburbs, the malls, the increasingly long commutes, the astronomical rise in housing prices. Blame single parents, working parents, stay-at-home moms, absent fathers. Blame our overscheduled lives, our overscheduled children, our inability to carry on a conversation, our desire to befriend our own progeny. Blame Republicans, Democrats, failed urban policy, failed farm subsidies, failed educational reform. Blame everything and everyone, because the causes are deep and widespread, easy to pinpoint, hard to pin down.* One thing, however, is clear: We eat quickly and tastelessly, and when we do, it's rarely with each other.†

---

* In his book *The Omnivore's Dilemma*, Michael Pollan blames the "industrial food chain," "which breaks the family down into its various demographics and markets separately to each one." His point is that corporations have a vested interest in splitting apart the family at mealtime because in doing so they can get each individual to consume more.

† According to the U.S. Census Bureau, 65% of children aged 6 to 17 had dinner every day with at least one parent, although this statistic is hard to believe and misleading. For one thing, according to a recent *Los Angeles Times* poll, the

In my home, my children's eating habits have declined since the days my wife mashed her own steamed carrots for baby food. Since then she has fought a valiant but often losing battle on the side of fresh fruits and vegetables, healthy vegetarian entrées, the food pyramid. These days, my children prefer beige foods, white foods, anything microwaveable. My son practically lived on Annie's macaroni and cheese for nearly two years. Now he will eat pasta with pesto, though not with tomato sauce. My daughter, on the other hand, will tolerate the latter but not the former. She prefers chicken, while my son eats only hot dogs. Neither likes cereal with milk, but my daughter adores milk and cereal (just not together) while my son can't stand either. Each day is a struggle to make healthy choices, a battle my wife fights alone, armed only with apple slices and baby carrots, whole wheat fusilli and free-range eggs.

Several days after my return from Kansas City, she asks if I will make black bean burritos for dinner. It has been months since I've cooked anything, and nearly a year since I made burritos. It was at one time one of our favorite dishes, taught to me by an old friend in Iowa City who insisted on sharp knives and fresh ingredients. The beans, he stressed, should be soaked overnight before cooking at least five hours over a very low flame, the beans scraped as they stick to the bottom of the pot so they end up mashed and

---

numbers are significantly lower for working parents (and for white parents). In addition, given that two-thirds of our children are raised by single parents, fewer than 25% eat with *both* parents on any given night even if the Census Bureau figures are to be believed. Further, the Census Bureau relies on self-reporting for its data, which should be taken with a very large grain of salt. Other experts, such as restaurateur Alice Waters, have put the number of families that eat together regularly at 33%. Nearly all the working parents I spoke to when I was writing this book told me they never ate dinner with their families except on the weekend.

pulpy, a thick black paste. My wife has already bought the ingredients, intending to make the dish herself, which offends me slightly since I think of the burritos in a proprietary way.

It's early on a Saturday in late summer. Too late for vacation, too soon for school. Outside, the sun burns a slow hazy arc across the sky. The kind of weather that finds dogs lying beneath picnic tables and kids running through sprinklers. My own kids have ridden their bicycles down the block, an anachronism in a time of supervised playdates and GPS devices, possible only because we live on an L-shaped cul-de-sac with close friends at the other end who call my wife when our kids arrive. It's a measure of freedom that my children cherish and I took for granted when I was their age.

Though I don't have time to soak the beans overnight, I boil them and let them sit for an hour, then drain and refill the small pot with enough water to cover the beans. I dice a medium onion and add two cloves of crushed garlic to the pot while the water heats. When it boils again, I turn the flame down and cover the pot. Then I go outside to find my kids.

My wife is weeding the garden. This is new, this weeding thing. In Iowa City I kept a small garden, growing tomatoes and various herbs, but my wife, who was raised in Idaho, was averse to anything having to do with the earth or nature, as if in reaction to her agrarian roots. When we first met, she told me she was from Seattle, embarrassed, she later admitted, to confess a rural identity she did her best to disguise, wearing bright red MAC lipstick, baby doll dresses, clunky shoes, and funky glasses. She kept her hair, in those days, in a blunt pageboy cut, modeling herself after the silent screen star Louise Brooks. As a boy from Long Island who had spent most of his life trying to flee, I understood the desire to remake oneself.

"We have aphids," she says.

She wears a tank top. The sun and heat have brought out the freckles across her arms and back. A redhead, my wife doesn't tan; instead, her skin is flushed like a woman in the throes of passion.

"Sounds scary," I say.

"They eat the roses."

"Since when have you become a horticulturalist?"

She smiles, muckle-mouthed, one incisor peering through the gap.

"You know what Dorothy Parker said about horticulture."

I realize this is the first conversation we have had about something other than the kids or work in weeks.

"Anyway," she adds, "I'd rather do it myself than pay Eddie."

This is also new, the Yankee parsimony. When we met, my wife couldn't balance a checkbook and saw no need to do it; her expenditures were trivial and often ephemeral: bath salts, body mist, henna. She frequently suffered from shopping bulimia, bingeing and then returning everything the next day. She had expensive tastes, but lacked the wherewithal to follow through.

I can hear our neighbor's lawn mower, and see him through the thick brush that separates our properties.* He and his wife work freelance producing television commercials, and their daughter uses our backyard as a shortcut to the high school. On the other side, our neighbors are an entomologist and a legal recruiter. Their daughter recently graduated and is now pursuing a career as a ballet dancer. Our little cul-de-sac boasts its fair share of creative types, and its fair share of tragedy: Across the street the mother of two young daughters recently died of an aneurysm at

---

* Though "good fences make good neighbors," as the poet wrote, the cheap wire fence that separates our properties has long disintegrated, and the straggly line of stones that marks the boundary would hardly keep out a dog, let alone a neighbor.

the age of forty, collapsing on the staircase in the middle of an afternoon, reminding us all of the brevity and randomness of life.

"When are the kids coming back?" I ask.

My wife shrugs. One strap of her tank top slips down her shoulder.

"Want to go inside?" I ask.

She smiles. She knows what's on my mind. "I have to finish gardening," she says.

"You can finish later."

"I can't."

She is punishing me, I know, for the weeks and months of indifference. I can hardly blame her, but the rejection hurts. I huff back inside to my beans, stirring them with a little too much vigor so that brackish water spills onto the burners, then evaporates with an angry hiss, leaving behind an odor like smoldering aluminum.

But the warmth of the kitchen and the smell of garlic soon distract me. I stir the pot again, this time more slowly, with more care. The beans are soft, though far from finished. I pick up the avocados my wife has purchased and squeeze their flesh, feeling them yield, just ripe, ideal for guacamole. She has purchased my favorite chips—Huskies "restaurant style"—and my favorite salsa—Mrs. Renfro's—and they sit on the counter next to a can of pitted extra large black olives, which my children eat as if they were candy. Beside the olives are two fat tomatoes. Although Christine hates them, she knows the tomatoes in the garden have yet to yield fruit. I check the refrigerator, and there's cilantro, lemons, sour cream, scallions, tortillas, and a package of grated Monterey Jack cheese. Everything, in short, for perfect black bean burritos.

Over the next couple hours I read the newspaper, check my e-mail, surf the Internet, play my guitar, and always return to the beans. It is a delicious, and rare, opportunity for mischief, but I have no one with whom to share it. My wife remains outdoors and my children with their friends, leaving me alone to pad through the house. I plug my iPod into a set of kitchen speakers, filling the room with music. I scrape the bottom of the pot and add a healthy dose of salt to the beans. I put on water to boil for rice, then make the guacamole. As I am mashing an avocado with the back of a fork, my wife comes into the kitchen. The song goes: *Every time I see you baby / I get down on my knees and pray*. It is one of our favorites, a song we danced to years ago at the 620 Club in Iowa City, our first date. She thought I was gay; I thought she was hot; and at four in the morning our stars aligned.

She takes my hand and asks, "Friends?"

"Friends," I say.

Then she kisses me lightly and says, "Smells good."

I add a dollop of sour cream and a couple tablespoons of Mrs. Renfro's to the avocados, squeeze a lime, chop some cilantro, but hold off on the tomatoes in deference to my wife. Instead, I set them aside along with some diced black olives, a red pepper, and the scallions, each in its own bowl.

My son thumps into the kitchen and asks what's for dinner. He's wearing a Yankees jersey, a Dodgers cap, and a pair of basketball sneakers without socks. I tell him, and he says, "Yeah!" as if his favorite team has just won the pennant. His sister follows him, and she asks, "Daddy, can I stir the beans?" I hand her the ladle, then guide her hand carefully over the pot. "It's hot," I caution. "I *know*," she says, as if she can't believe my stupidity. We taste a couple of beans together.

"More salt," says Lulu. Then she wanders over to the iPod and selects "Le Freak" by Chic.

Though my children are obsessed with iTunes, Lulu's tastes run toward old disco and new dance music, Hilary Duff, Avril

Lavigne, and Cheetah Girls, while Simon likes '80s rock—the Clash, the Ramones—and anything new with loud guitars and drums. Both agree that the B-52's are cool, and neither understands my love of the Talking Heads. When we drive somewhere, we play "Name That Song" as the iPod shuffles through its lineup. They are remarkably conversant with the names of bands, songs, and albums, surprising guests and family members with their knowledge of obscure synth-pop bands and minor new wave groups. In this respect they are, as my wife notes, my children.

Now she enlists their help to set the table, which causes a minor flare-up, but nothing I can't ignore to the disco beat. I take the rice from the stove and set it on the table. I give the beans a final stir, then shut off the flame. I heat a large cast-iron skillet and warm a tortilla, sprinkle it with cheese, then add a big dollop of beans, which are now a thick black paste with a few discrete beans.

One of the best things about black bean burritos is that they can be customized for picky eaters who do not like cilantro, salsa, guacamole, or scallions. The tortillas I roll for my children have only beans and cheese inside them. The one I roll for my wife lacks scallions and, of course, tomatoes. Mine has everything.

We eat in a noisy silence filled with chewing, chomping, slurping, and sucking. It is the kind of silence that fills a dinner table between people who are as comfortable with each other as an old pair of shoes. The kind of silence, I realize, I rarely hear anymore. Finally, my son speaks.

"Can I have another?"

This from a boy who rarely touches dinner, who has to be cajoled to eat a doughnut, who defines the word "beanpole." He has cleaned his plate before I have finished half of mine. Of course I will make him another burrito. I feel like laughing for joy. I get up and return to the stove. "Me, too," says my daughter.

"You haven't finished the one on your plate," says my wife.

"But I know I'm going to want another."

"No problem," I say.

I fire up the skillet, then roll two more burritos. When I bring them to the table, my daughter lets out an enormous belch.

"Lulu!" my wife scolds her in mock horror.

"What?" she asks.

"It's not polite to belch."

"It is in Japan."

"Well, we don't live in Japan."

But it's too late, Lulu has set off a belching contest. Simon tries to outdo her, but for a six-year-old girl, she's a remarkable belcher. The contest ends only when my wife stops laughing long enough to put her hand over Lulu's mouth.

"You're going to break a rib," she says.

Lulu looks just credulous enough to stop. "Really, Mommy?" she asks.

"No," I say. "But you might not be invited to dine with the Queen of England."

"Does the Queen like burritos?"

It's a good question, and one to which I'm forced to admit I don't know the answer.

"I bet she'd like Dad's," says Simon. "Everyone does."

Christine smiles at me, and I know what she's thinking: Where did they come from, these fabulous creatures who amaze us with their dead-on observations and their sitcom antics? It seems like five minutes ago they were slurping baby food from a tiny spoon, and now they're lecturing us about our tastes in music.

Over their protests we make the kids clear the table, bringing the dishes to the sink, where Christine rinses them and places them in the dishwasher. Simon claims he has to go to the bathroom, and Christine lets him go. Lulu follows him upstairs. I tell my wife it's an old trick, one my sister used to pull on our parents. She shrugs, not the disciplinarian, and says he's earned a break. I don't disagree. Instead, I help her finish cleaning the kitchen, wrap the scallions and peppers in cellophane, leave the beans to cool, scrape the rice into a plastic container.

We work quietly, side by side, with the practiced rhythm of a long-married couple, as if dinner together is a time-honored ritual, sacred and esteemed, instead of an occurrence as rare as a lunar eclipse.

"You seemed happy tonight," Christine says when the last dish is put away.

"I like to cook," I say, and I do. The Zen of it. The calm precision of measuring and chopping. The alchemy of stirring and heating. Unlike my jobs, which nourish my family in their own way, putting a plate before my children is direct, visible, and tangible. The results are immediate and clear. Working is abstract and conceptual, while cooking is concrete and corporeal. Work takes me away; cooking brings me home. The former is necessary but not sufficient, the latter essential and primordial. One is absence, the other presence. On his deathbed, no one has prayed for more work. Plenty have died from hunger, however.

I see myself then in my most critical eye: my Type A personality, my restlessness, impatience, and constant dissatisfaction. My multiple employers a reflection of my inability to stay put, to live in the moment, to appreciate the things in this world. My absence—both literal and figurative—from my family's life as I hunt down the next dollar, shrug off the next accomplishment, check my e-mail when I should be checking my son's homework. But I also see the beginnings of a plan, my own 12-step program toward recovery.

"What would our life be like if I were home for dinner every night?" I ask.

"Every night?" Christine repeats, with something between in-credulity and astonishment.

"Well, not every night. I have to teach one night a week. And it would be nice to go out on a Friday or Saturday sometimes. Five nights a week."

"And would you cook?"

Now it's my turn to be incredulous. "Not every night."

"How about half the nights?"

"Two and a half nights a week?" I calculate quickly: If I made dinner both weekend nights, I would almost make my quota. But that still leaves half an unaccounted-for night, and assumes we don't go out for dinner on any weekend. Could I find another half-night between flying to Kansas City, teaching evening classes, and an interminable commute? Could I get home early enough to start the water boiling, chop the vegetables, shuck the corn, marinate the tofu? Given my current schedule, it seems impossible. On the other hand, to continue as I have been is simply implausible, in-comprehensible, unbearable. Once I walked my son to preschool; now I can't recall his teacher's name. I don't know my daughter's classmates, and haven't attended a holiday concert in two years. I have never planned their birthday party or selected a gift. At the holidays, I am as surprised as they to find what Santa or the Hanukkah man has left under the tree. I don't fear my children will become drug addicts or computer hackers, but missing dinner means missing a large part of their lives, the part they are living right now. How many years do I have left before they ignore me, walk behind me, hang up the phone when I come near? Already, the time has gone so fast it leaves me breathless. In a matter of moments, they will be gone.

I am not a reckless person, but I am a desperate one. What I am about to do will change my life in ways I cannot know, or choose to ignore. For years I have speeded everything up, accumulated and agglomerated, stepped on the fast track and let it whip me about. Now, I will force myself to deliberately slow down, to pay attention to the most important details around me. Like the poets I used to read in Iowa City, I will narrow my focus to the essential elements until I find a greater truth—or madness.

Here, then, is the promise I make to Christine, Simon, and Lulu, and to myself: For this next school year I will be home for dinner at least five nights a week, sharing equally in the shopping, prepping, cooking, and cleaning.* Instead of stuffing a taco into my mouth in the back of the train, I will sauté chicken and peppers for my own fajitas. Instead of dining alone, I will dine with my family. Instead of Absent Dad, I will be Nourishing Dad.

A simple plan, with clear boundaries, the kind of rules a child could love: Dinner with Dad, five nights a week.

---

* In Westport, the school year begins the first week of September and ends the third week in June.

Skewered

"**W**ake up, wake up, wake up." I shake my son in his bed, the light streaming in behind me, a new day dawning.

"Go away, Dad!" he says.

"What do you want for breakfast?"

"Nothing. Go away."

"Come on. I'll make you scrambled eggs. Scrambled eggs and a bagel! Won't that be good?"

"I hate eggs. Go away!" He pushes my hand from his hair and buries his head beneath the blanket.

"Simon, so help me God, if you don't get up now, I'm going to take away your PlayStation for a week!"

And so it goes, until, finally I drag him kicking and screaming downstairs and sit him next to his sister at the kitchen table.

It's September. School is back in session. Backpacks, book bags, and lunch boxes sit on the counter; new shoes line the door; shiny jackets hang from a hook. Change is in the air. For one thing, I've stopped leaving before the sun rises, at least on days when I'm working at home. For another, I'm working at home, at least a couple days a week. If my kids notice, however, they haven't said anything—at least nothing nice.

I walk them to the bus stop, then watch them race up the steps and to their seats when the bus arrives. I linger on the corner while the mothers share gossip, feeling slightly self-conscious—a man in a world of stay-at-home moms. "Vacation?" a neighbor asks.

"Working at home," I explain.

"Does your wife know?" She laughs, and I join her, not sure if that's the proper response. It's not as if I am the only man who has ever taken his children to the bus stop or taken a day to work at home. Yet it feels slightly illegal, like playing hooky and dodging the truant officer.

We walk together back up the street, and she bids me farewell at our mailbox. "Enjoy your day off," she says. I don't correct her.

For the last few years my dual careers as a law professor and partner at a law firm, then professor and "special counsel" to a media insurance company, have meant sixty- to eighty-hour weeks with little time to write and no time for my wife or children. Like a descent into bankruptcy, the transformation to workaholic was gradual, then all at once. I had too many options, too many choices, and lacked the discipline to just say no. As my salary increased, my appetite grew, until I needed every dollar I was making and lived from paycheck to paycheck. I was trapped in a cycle of my own making from which the chances of escape appeared dim. But I could stop the carousel if I wanted. I could get off.

Perhaps I might have managed if I were single, fifteen years younger, had not yet built up a tolerance to caffeine. Maybe if my daughter hadn't become her own little person, interested in the lyrics to songs even when the words went *I'm your boogie man / I'm your boogie man / Turn me on.* But now that I knew what I was missing, I didn't want to miss it anymore.

I couldn't cook dinner, however, if I was commuting to Kansas City, where the insurance company for which I am special counsel is located. But when I announced my plans, the CEO wouldn't let me quit. There were client relationships to manage, year-end goals to be reached, and other, less drastic options available. If I didn't want to travel, I could work from home; there are conference calls and webcams, voice mail, e-mail, and overnight delivery. Although I was dubious, I hated to disappoint anyone. Plus, the fiscal reality had begun to set in, and continued employment, even if it meant working late nights at home, seemed like a lifeline. So I didn't quit—at least not yet.

When I return to the house, Christine seems surprised to see me.

"I thought you were going to the library," she says.

"I am. I just have to check my e-mail."

"My writing group is coming over at ten."

"I'll be gone in fifteen minutes."

"Okay." But she doesn't sound too happy about it.

"In case you haven't noticed, I live here, too," I say.

"I know. But I'm used to having the house to myself."

"Fine," I say, and retreat to my office to pout. Five minutes later, however, still steamed, I grab my laptop and leave, slamming the door behind me.

I drive too fast on the Post Road, where BMWs and Lexus SUVs compete with Audis, Saabs, and Volvo wagons. In my six-year-old Volkswagen I feel slightly slovenly, suddenly conscious that my car is small, dirty, and not this year's model. A month ago it would not have bothered me; now it no longer feels charming, but a reflection of my newly precarious financial state. I step on the gas and speed past a Mercedes convertible. Even if I don't have the slickest car on the road, I can still break the law.

When I arrive at the library, the parking lot is nearly empty. I walk from the bright sunshine into the cool hum of the air-conditioned lobby where a small café and several tables lend a genteel air to the brick and steel building. The librarians seem surprised to see me, and one of them asks if I need any help, as if I might have wandered in accidentally. I feel self-conscious telling her I'm working, and explain instead that I'm looking for the magazines. She directs me to the reading room.

I set up at a table near the window and work there most of the day, using the wireless network to send my e-mail. It's surprisingly pleasant. The reading room overlooks the Saugatuck River, and except for a few retirees who come to read the various newspapers, and one other man who, from the glimpses I catch of his résumé on his computer, appears to be job-hunting, I have the place to myself. I am reminded of the wonder of libraries, the fact that there are all these books available free for our asking and plenty of space to read them. There are even magazines, which I hardly ever consider purchasing but now pull hungrily from the shelves as if they might disappear.

I begin to think the library might be a perfect alternative to my home office, until I get a call on my cell phone from an underwriter in Kansas City. I have to abandon my laptop and walk outside to take the call, muffling the speaker with my hand so I won't be overheard. I'm vague about my whereabouts, and promise to call her back later with an answer to the questions she's just asked. Then I run quickly back to my computer, half-expecting it to be gone. But it's there, just as I left it, and I settle back into my seat, with barely a look from the craggy-faced geezer seated across from me.

In the afternoon, I get hungry. I buy a muffin and coffee, but it's not enough to stave off thoughts of dinner. Although it's only four-thirty, I consider shopping for food. I tell myself I've put in a productive eight hours of work, not counting the muffin break. If

I were punching the clock, it would be time to sign out. Of course, we live in a clockless society, where a man's worth is measured by his accessibility 24/7. What was once the close of the working day is now just the middle of a never-ending crunch. For a man who has been pulling eighty-hour weeks, a mere eight hours doesn't cut it; it's a warm-up, a toss-off, a dalliance with employment. In Japan, the day has barely begun.

The more I contemplate dinner, however, the harder it is to concentrate on work, until the thought of food practically drives me out the door.

Westport has at least six food markets, catering to different tastes and budgets. There's Stop & Shop, big, generic, and convenient. Shaw's is its nearest competitor, closer to town but smaller, with a more limited selection. Between the two is Balducci's, formerly Hay Day, with outrageous prices but the place to go for fancy prepared foods, cheese, and bread. Then there's Trader Joe's, a funky, inexpensive chain with great frozen and packaged foods. On the other side of the river, there's Wild Oats, an organic supermarket with prices to rival Balducci's, and Stew Leonard's, the famous food discounter.*

So much choice, so little time! Although few of us cook anymore,† there are more places than ever before to buy ingredients. Like our kitchens, our shopping carts overflow with unnecessary ingredients: designer mushrooms, organic rice, free-range tofu.

---

* This list doesn't even include the summer farmer's market, some outstanding local fish stores, and Penzeys, a great shop that sells only spices.

† According to the National Restaurant Association, Americans spent more than $470 billion dining out in 2005, which comprised nearly 50% of our total food budget, compared with 40.5% of our food budget in 2000 and 25% of our food budget in 1955.

You would think we were a land of macrobiotic vegetarian Continental gourmands instead of a country in the midst of a type 2 diabetes epidemic. Our national bird is the chicken nugget and our favorite vegetable the French fry. We can barely be bothered with cooking, let alone eating—which is why we enjoy our meals in front of the television, on the phone, in the car, and sometimes all three at once.

It is laziness, then, more than any specific plan, that brings me to Shaw's. On the way home from the library, it's an easy stop. I make the classic mistake of the novice shopper and do not bring a list, or even an idea of what I want to cook. Instead, I wander the aisles, hoping for inspiration. Perhaps because I am hungry myself, light-headed from the muffin, I find it hard to make a decision. Nothing strikes me as particularly desirable, except the candy bars, and I soon end up in a hyperglycemic daze before the shish kebabs.

This is a problem. First, Christine won't eat meat. Second, my kids will not eat grilled vegetables. Nevertheless, my mouth waters at the thought of barbecue. If I can't get Simon and Lulu to eat grilled onions, at least they ought to eat grilled chicken. I buy three kebabs. For Christine, I buy a package of veggie burgers. Six ears of corn, a bag of premade salad mix, and a loaf of bread. For dessert, a pint of Ben & Jerry's cookie dough ice cream. I am famished.

The express checkout line is agonizingly long, so I hop to a shorter line behind a woman with a full shopping cart. This turns out to be a mistake—not because of the quantity of food in the woman's cart, but because the cashier is unfamiliar with the various codes for fruits and vegetables. He looks them up in a plastic Rolodex next to his cash register. Meanwhile, two lines away, the express line moves with the speed of a small child on a sugar buzz. I grit my teeth, tap my feet, and push my cart back and forth—all to no avail. Clearly, I have missed the first lesson in supermarket strategy: Choose the line based on the checker's proficiency, not the number of carts.*

When I finally emerge, the horizon has turned an orange-yellow like something heavy and nuclear. I climb into my car and lock the doors.

I arrive home to an empty house. There is no note, and no sign of children. I try Christine on her cell phone, but she has a habit of leaving it behind, which I discover when I hear it ringing in the other room. I suddenly realize I don't know my own children's schedule, what they do, where they go. I feel like a man in a Lifetime television movie whose wife has fled to her sister's in Gainesville. I shuffle around the kitchen, not exactly sure what to do with myself. I call our neighbors, but they're not home either.

It strikes me then how peripheral I am in my family's life. Wherever they are, they didn't think to include or inform me. And why should they? My absence has been a constant for so long that it would be strange for them to account for me. Instead, they have gone on with their plans as they have every day—three of them and me, the odd one out.

By now it is six o'clock. Assuming they have to come home soon, I fire up the grill, a simple matter of adding charcoal and pressing "ignite." The grill was a housewarming gift from my brother and sister shortly after we moved. It arrived fully assembled from the hardware store, a gleaming Weber that seemed too shiny to actually use. Since then, the few meals I have cooked have been on it. As with most men, the barbecue is my domain, although I really have no idea what I'm doing. The cookbooks that promise

---

* My ignorance might be excused based on the fact that the average working man spends less than four minutes a day grocery shopping—not a lot of time to learn the nuances of line management.

mastering the art of barbecuing sit unopened on the shelf, partly because I have no time to read them and partly because I wonder how much "art" there really is to barbecuing. What could be more basic than placing meat over fire, something our cave ancestors must have done without the benefit of marinades, smokers, or tongs.

By 6:30 P.M. the coals are ashen white. Still no sign of my family. The slightest note of worry has crept into my mind. I imagine traffic accidents, emergency room visits, sudden hospitalizations. Yet even without a cell phone I think my wife would have called me. Mostly, I'm concerned about the coals, and how long they will hold their temperature. At 6:45 I decide to start cooking, reasoning that I can always reheat the shish kebabs when they return.

But it's no fun cooking for no one. It reminds me of my first year in Iowa, before I met my wife. With a big kitchen and lots of time, I often set out to make something tasty from my limited repertoire: stir-fry, fettuccine Alfredo, Spanish rice. I'd end up with much more food than I needed, and after two or three days of leftovers would toss the rest of it out. Eating alone reinforced how isolated I was in the Iowa cornfields, and frightened me because it seemed to portend my future as a writer. I tried to avoid it when I could, and took to having dinner parties or inviting myself to a friend's house to eat.

The shish kebabs cook quickly. I leave the veggie burgers off the grill because a microwaved reheated veggie patty holds about as little appeal for me as I think it will for Christine. She can fry it in a pan when she returns—if she returns. I do not cook the corn, or make a salad, and the bread remains in its wrapper. I carry my plate to the family room, turn on the television, and eat my shish kebab on the sofa alone.

Finally, about 7:30, when I've nearly decided to call the police, my family arrives.

They pull up the driveway in Christine's car, and my heart thumps hard in my chest. Both kids leap out of the car, followed by my wife, who is carrying a large tote bag.

"Daddy, Daddy!" says Lulu, running toward me. "We had a picnic on the beach."

I am torn between love for this little girl and anger at all of them for forgetting about me.

"A picnic," I say. "With who?"

"The PTA picnic," says Christine. "Didn't you get my e-mail?"

"What e-mail?"

"The one I forwarded you. Before we left."

Apparently, in my eagerness to shop for dinner, I overlooked a last-minute message from my wife about a back-to-school picnic on the beach. Never mind that she sent it to me about five minutes before they left. Never mind that I received the original e-mail and flyer but ignored them both, not being accustomed to school outings, like some reclusive shut-in.

"Did you have dinner?" I ask, stupidly.

"Oh, I'm sorry," says Christine, kissing me gently on the cheek, my empty plate telling her everything she needs to know.

"I thought we could have shish kebabs."

"We'll have them tomorrow," she offers.

"I already cooked them."

"We'll reheat them."

"What time was the picnic?" I ask, redirecting my wrath toward the PTA.

Christine says it began at five, although they were late. They arrived just in time, however, to eat grilled burgers, hot dogs, and veggie burgers in the balmy breeze off Long Island sound.

"Were there any fathers?" I ask.

"A couple," she says.

"Two?"

"Rob was there."

"How do they expect fathers to make these things?"

Christine shrugs. We both know suburban life is timed to the stay-at-home parent. From the back-to-school "open house" scheduled on a Tuesday at 9:30 A.M., to parent-teacher conferences scheduled at two in the afternoon, to holiday concerts planned for the late morning, no one is thinking about the working parent—at least not very hard. Most of the parents who commute into Manhattan can't get home in time for dinner, let alone a barbecue on the beach, so why try to accommodate their schedule? It would only make it more difficult for the other parents, who would have to get babysitters, and for teachers, who would have to work fourteen-hour days. Of course, like a self-fulfilling prophecy, pretty soon we are all living like a television show from the 1950s.

"Anyway," says Christine. "The kids had a great time."

I look at them circling around the kitchen floor, Lulu fending off Simon's advances with an empty paper towel roll like a kitchen gladiator.

"It was my turn to make dinner," I say, one last attempt at sympathy.

"We didn't know. Remember, you stormed out this morning."

Communication, they say, begins at home, while you still have time—and an audience.

"I'm sorry," I say.

"So am I." She slips her hand into mine. "Come on, kids," she says. "Bedtime."

"Aw, Mom!" says Simon.

"Last one up is a rotten avocado."

Lulu drops her weapon and races for the stairs. She's quick, but not as quick as her father, who overtakes her on the first step and carries her triumphantly into the bathroom.

"I really wanted shish kebab," she says to me as I put tooth-paste on her toothbrush.

"Really?"

"Can we have it tomorrow night?"

"Sure."

"Okay."

I watch her brush, the bristles rubbing the empty spaces where teeth should be.

"Daddy," she says when she's done, her moon face looking up at me. "What's a shish kebab?"

A Tale of
Two Pizzas

Westport, Connecticut, the actress Joanne Woodward writes, "is a place where the rich and famous live side by side with the descendants of the original Yankee farmers. . . . Eclectic and cosmopolitan . . . [it] has become a mecca for those who are traditionally untraditional."

Perhaps Ms. Woodward's observations were accurate in the 1950s (although she wrote her words in 2000), but these days Westport is just another wealthy suburb with good schools and nice homes, mostly indistinguishable from hundreds of other towns with their Gaps and Starbucks and Banana Republics. Once upon a time, I am told, Westport had its share of independent bookstores and movie theaters, but even those are gone, replaced by a sprawling Barnes & Noble and the usual movie megaplexes. The downtown boasts a Talbots, Restoration Hardware, Williams-Sonoma, and Brooks Brothers, and the extended shopping district along the Post Road includes CompUSA, Sports Authority, Home Depot, Staples, Circuit City, and many others.* Cosmopolitan, perhaps, but only if you consider that these days you can find the same stores in most American cities.

As for "untraditional," the town is overwhelmingly white,[†] with a significant minority of Jewish families (maybe this is what Ms. Woodward means when she says Westport is "eclectic"). It votes mostly Democratic and tends to be one of the more liberal places in Connecticut, which means residents don't object to paying taxes as long as the average SAT score remains above 1100. Whereas Westport was once "an established center for creative people," according to Woody Klein, author of *Westport, Connecticut: The Story of a New England Town's Rise to Prominence,* with its share of writers, artists, and editors, that is no longer the case. Indeed, it is rare to meet a working parent in Westport who is not employed in the financial services, legal, or advertising businesses. Many commute to Stamford, where large financial companies like UBS have their corporate headquarters, and others travel farther south to Greenwich, which has become the de facto home of the hedge fund industry.

The median home in Westport sold for $933,000 in 2004. In this, Westport was actually less expensive than a number of other southern Connecticut towns: Greenwich ($1.5 million), New Canaan ($1.1 million), and Darien ($982,000). The *average* sales price was several hundred thousand dollars higher in all these

---

* In *Bobos in America,* David Brooks describes the loss of local businesses and industry to the relentless march of upscale suburbanization, which is exemplified by Westport, a town that used to be more notable as a summer retreat for city residents than as an expensive commuting suburb. Drive around the town and you'll see the evidence everywhere: McMansions where cottages once stood.

† In the fall of 1995, according to town records, fewer than 1% of Westport students were black.

towns, reflecting the number of extremely large and expensive houses that drive the average price higher than the median.* Westport's housing prices rank significantly below those in dozens of towns on the West Coast (particularly around San Francisco and Los Angeles), and plenty of comparable towns in suburban New York and New Jersey such as Great Neck ($1.2 million), Short Hills ($1.1 million), Rye ($1.1 million), Pound Ridge ($994,000), and Manhasset ($984,000), to name just a few. Local taxes also tend to be about half those imposed by towns in Westchester and Nassau counties, and there are more affordable housing pockets around the train station, the interstate, and the schools. In short, Westport is an expensive place to live, but not that expensive compared to other towns with top-ranked public schools that are within commuting distance of New York, L.A., San Francisco, and even Chicago.

When we moved from New York City, Westport seemed like a veritable bargain. For the sale price of our two-bedroom apartment, we purchased a five-bedroom, three-and-a-half-bath home on an acre of land. In addition, we saved the annual cost of private school, which in Manhattan can run twenty-five to thirty thousand dollars a year per child. Though the commute was about twice what it would have been from Port Washington or Larchmont, two other towns we seriously considered, the same money bought us a significantly larger house with four times as much land and half the property taxes. We felt blessed by our good fortune, grateful that we had bought (and sold) our apartment in

According to a story on NPR in March 2005, older houses in Westport were torn down to make room for bigger homes at the rate of more than one per week. In Fairfield County, Westport's teardown rate was second only to Greenwich's. A popular website, Westportnow.com, maintains an interactive map detailing the "Teardown of the Day."

New York at the right time, and happy that we would have more space, excellent public schools, friendly neighbors, a backyard, and a garage.

The one thing we did not consider, and could not purchase, was time. Perhaps foolishly, I imagined I would continue teaching, commuting to New York two or three days a week, and writing at home. Thus, the two-hour commute to lower Manhattan did not overly concern me; I could read and work on the train and enjoy a leisurely beginning (and end) to my day. But the financial stress of living in an expensive suburb soon put the lie to those plans. Although I earned a decent salary as a law professor, and some money as a freelance writer, it was not enough to maintain a home in an expensive suburb without a second income. Because Christine and I had made the decision that she would stay home with the children for as long as possible, it was up to me to earn that second income. Thus, even after I transitioned to full-time teaching, I continued to practice law. My legal work took me to New York, and then Kansas City, with increasing frequency, and working at home became a mythic and forgotten daydream.

Each morning, as I boarded the 6:46 or 7:15 for the seventy-minute train trip in to Manhattan, followed by the thirty-minute subway ride and crosstown walk to Tribeca, I wondered whether I could ever become inured to this trek. The hundred or so other commuters at Green's Farms station seemed deadened to the hardships of early-morning risings, wind-whipped platforms, overcrowded and stinking cars, and the indignities wreaked upon us by the scheduling failures of Metro-North. I wondered how they grew old without rebelling against the system, chucking it all for a place in Vermont, driving themselves to work in the morning. Most of all, I wondered how they got home in time for dinner.

In fact, most of them did not—at least not with their families. The men I met at the station, with very few exceptions, never sat down to a family meal on a weekday. Instead, their wives fed the children, then waited for them, or left them their meals to reheat. The few exceptions were the traders who worked in Greenwich or Stamford and whose days began earlier and commutes were significantly shorter, or who managed, through BlackBerry and cell phone, to stay in touch even while at the dinner table.

Though a handful of women commuted every morning, my unscientific survey* put the figure at lower than 15 percent. Most of the commuters were men, and most had wives at home (at least if my random conversations are considered a fair sampling). I suspect few women in Westport commuted to jobs in Manhattan because the commute was so much longer than from some of the towns in Westchester County, and many people chose to live in Westport if they knew only one parent would be commuting. Still, there is a definite trend among working women to return to the home, forsaking the careers they fought so hard to establish, and this trend is more pronounced in Westport. Most of my wife's friends had graduate degrees, careers, commutes, before they gave up their day jobs for the more full-time job of raising their kids in the suburbs. Now their energies are directed toward the school, the home, the PTA, and their children.[†]

---

* On October 31, for example, there were 62 men and 5 women waiting for the 6:46 A.M. On November 2, I counted 85 men and 10 women waiting for the 7:15 A.M. On November 3, coming home on the 6:30 P.M., there were 102 men and 12 women.

† The school, for example, makes no effort even to mask these preferences, designating "room mothers" and "art-smart moms." Step inside a classroom, or a lunchroom, as I have done, and you might see one father among dozens of mothers. At my daughter's first-grade "graduation," I was one of only two fathers to attend.

Combating the stereotypes takes a concerted effort, and not just because of the psychological issues. Who's going to raise the kids? Who's going to pick them up at the bus stop, ferry them to their activities, help them with their homework, cook dinner for them? If both parents are working, this is an arduous task, and often involves paying someone else to perform some or all of these activities. Unless both parents are doctors or lawyers or bankers, the cost of hiring someone can equal or exceed the after-tax salary of the lower-earning parent—it certainly did in our case. Thus, good capitalists that we are, we divide and conquer, maximizing our earning potential while minimizing our family strife, and sub-scribing to the assembly-line model of parenting.

Of course, plenty of families don't have these choices, but since the end of the 1990s, the number of families in which both parents are working and the number of women in the workforce with children has actually decreased, suggesting that more and more women are choosing to stay home.

As I drove to the train station, I wondered again whether stay-ing in the New York region was the right choice for us. For a month in the winter, Christine and I had flirted with the idea of moving to Kansas City, but eventually decided against it. It wasn't that we loved Connecticut so much, it was what Connecticut of-fered us that made moving so difficult. Within fifty miles of our home in Westport we had my parents and brother, who loved our children and could always be counted on to help when we needed them. Three hours north we had my sister, her husband, and my nephew, who lived outside Boston. Christine's father and most of her family, in contrast, lived in northern Idaho, where I was un-likely to find a job, and where I doubted we could ever assimilate.

But we didn't need to live in Westport. There were cheaper towns farther north, in New Jersey, on Long Island. None had public schools with the same reputation as Westport's, but perhaps that was a trade-off. More time with Dad in exchange for fewer AP classes in high school. Less financial stress in exchange for a lower acceptance rate at Harvard. There were no perfect solutions, only choices, each requiring a sacrifice in one form or another.

A week after the ill-fated barbecue, the parking lot at Williams-Sonoma is filled with SUVs and late-model cars. I squeeze into a space between a behemoth Lincoln Navigator and an equally huge Toyota Sequoia. You would think the drivers were hauling logs across the tundra. But the car seats in the back of both trucks are a dead giveaway the cargo is something smaller, and more animate. I sidestep my way out of my door, scraping against the Sequoia, practically holding my breath until I reach the sidewalk.

Williams-Sonoma is a veritable temple to cooking, a shrine to food preparation. Nothing in the store, however, looks as if it should actually be used in a kitchen without a permit. There are pots that gleam like silver, utensils whose true purpose must be divined, machines too frightening to encounter alone in a dark room. The store buzzes with shoppers, foodies hoping for inspiration, the right-sized slotted spoon, a French press. I pass an espresso maker that is on sale for three thousand dollars. Next to it, a set of copper pots on closeout for twenty-five hundred. A sales clerk gaily describes it to a striking blonde as the ultimate in cookware. The woman nods, and I surmise that the word "ultimate" means a lot more to her than "cookware."

When did cooking become a contact sport, with its televised competitions and celebrity chefs, its twenty-five-thousand-dollar ovens and space age pots? We shell out more money at restaurants than we do on the raw materials, yet we are obsessed with finding the perfect nonstick pan. In the same way, we have never been more sports and exercise obsessed, yet have never been fatter. We have never absorbed more literature, yet been less literate. It seems to me we can measure a civilization's collapse by the inverse relationship between its obsessions and its commitments, how much time it spends talking rather than doing.

I do not linger. In the back, I find the bread maker I have come to purchase, a birthday present from my parents. I am at the point in my life where my parents ask me what I want for my birthday, then send me out to buy it and write me a check to reimburse me. Of course, one might ask why I—a forty-something-year-old man—am still getting birthday presents from my parents, but that is another story. I ask a clerk for help, and she points out one that looks sturdy and expensive, the ultimate in bread machines. Since I am not paying, I say I will take it. At least I know I have plans to use it.

My brother is coming for dinner, and the truth is I want to impress him. My brother is a bit of a foodie himself. A bachelor, a Manhattan doctor, he frequents some of the best restaurants in New York courtesy of drug reps and a wealthy circle of friends. In my family, the boys got the food genes, while my sister subsists on a diet of Cheerios, Diet Coke, and Dunkin' decaf.

The clerk asks if I want the bread machine wrapped, and since it is a birthday present—albeit for myself—I say that I do. I carry it back to my car and squeeze into my front seat, placing the present next to me, then drive home.

Lulu races to the door when she sees the gift. "Did you get me something?" she asks.

"No. I got myself a present."

"Daaaad," she cries.

"Want to see what it is? You can help me."

"Okay," says Lulu, who is easily diverted, amused, charmed, unlike her far more intense brother.

We unwrap the gift on the kitchen table. It shimmers like something alive. "What is it?" Lulu asks.

"I'm going to make pizza," I say.

"Pizza! Can I twirl it?"

I'm not sure there's going to be any twirling, but I tell her we can try. I explain to Lulu the machine will help us make the dough, but we can make the pizza by hand together. We read the recipe booklet, then carefully measure out the ingredients. Lulu is disappointed to hear that the dough will take nearly an hour to rise, but I am amazed at the simplicity of the whole process: Throw some ingredients into a Teflon pan, press a button, and walk away. My experience with mixing and kneading has been messy, frustrating, and usually uneven. In Iowa City, it took days to clean the counters of encrusted dough. Weeks later, I would still find hardened bits between the counters, wedged into cracks in the floor, beside the refrigerator. Although my own grandfather had been a baker, I decided I lacked his gene for yeast. I was a boiler, not a sifter. I left the baking to Christine.

Now, while the machine goes to work, Lulu and I grate some mozzarella, which means that I grate it and she eats the errant pieces. Then we make a simple pizza sauce with a can of crushed tomatoes, some garlic cloves, oregano, basil, salt, and sugar. We let this cook on the stove on a slow simmer.

"What about toppings?" I ask.

"Marshmallows!" says Lulu.

"I don't think so," I say.

I am the only one who likes mushrooms, but we all like olives, so that's an easy choice. I decide to make one olive pizza and another pizza with garlic, peppers, and onions. Lulu loses interest and flees for the family room while I chop a red and a green pepper.

The setting sun casts the kitchen in a red glow. Dire Straits plays on a pair of speakers mounted above the cabinets. Christine ventures in, takes a whiff, gives me a kiss. I open the machine's door and poke the dough with an index finger. It makes me giggle, as if I am touching the Pillsbury Doughboy. Something jiggly, warm, sentient.

There's a honk from outside, and I hear my kids shout, "Uncle Adam! Uncle Adam!" Simon bounds down the stairs with the force of a buffalo.

My brother enters the house with Lulu in his arms. Dark and handsome, he is the perfect uncle, spoiling his niece and nephew with toys, movies, sporting events, and frequent visits. He swings Lulu around, then sets her on the ground.

"I'm making pizza!" she says.

"You are?"

"Dad and me."

"What kind?"

"Pizza with marshmallows!"

I wink at my brother, and he gives me a hug. My brother is several inches shorter than me but more muscular in the chest and arms. His hugs always feel like something permanent.

Simon grabs his arm and pulls him in the direction of his PlayStation. Adam looks back at me, and I tell him dinner will be ready in about twenty minutes.

I divide the dough and give half to Lulu. I show her how to stretch it, flattening it on the counter with her hands, pushing at the edges to stretch it out. When the dough is about the diameter of a basketball, we try tossing it in the air. Lulu's disk lands on her elbow and nearly slips to the floor. We try it again, but it won't stretch the way we've seen real pizza guys do it. Lulu seems disappointed, until I lay the dough flat on a heavily floured pizza paddle and let her spread the tomato sauce over it.

"Quickly," I encourage her. I know from past experience that the longer the dough sits on the paddle, the harder it will be to slide off.

Lulu spoons sauce over her oblong-shaped pizza. When she is done, the two of us sprinkle mozzarella and olives over the sauce. I carry the pizza to the oven and, with a quick jerk, slip it off the paddle and onto a pizza stone. A few olives fall into the oven, sizzling against the hot metal, but otherwise the transfer is successful.

I set about making the next pizza for the adults, but Lulu has lost interest and runs off to find Uncle Adam.

Our kitchen is small, the appliances dated. We don't have a fancy six-burner stove or double wall oven like some of our wealthier neighbors. Our single refrigerator/freezer is not nearly large enough for the entire family. Someday, Christine and I dream of a renovation—a giant island with recessed burners, a double sink, stainless-steel appliances, an ice maker. But as I remove the second pizza from the oven, the kitchen feels perfect: neither too big nor too small, neither too old nor too new. A family kitchen meant for cooking, not admiring, designed for eating, not a magazine. The kind of kitchen where my brother can enter carrying both my son and my daughter in his arms and plunk them into their seats without ceremony, without concern, with nothing but love.

"Uncle Adam! Uncle Adam!" they call. "Sit next to me!" He scrapes a chair across the floor and squeezes in next to both of them, his broad shoulders nearly brushing their cheeks. Lulu grasps his wrist, and Simon slips one foot on top of Adam's shoe. They are locked and loaded, ready for dough.

I serve the pizza, and for a moment there is nearly complete silence, the only sounds being the blowing of air across hot cheese and the chewing of crust.

"The best pizza," Simon concludes, "is homemade."

Hush Puppies

The bat hits the ball with the dull "bonk" of metal on cowhide. It curves, foul, down the right field line. I let out a sigh of relief.

If it's October, it must be baseball. Fall ball, as they call it in the suburbs. Once upon a time, autumn was reserved for football and the occasional lesser ovoid like soccer. These days, scholastic sports have spilled into all three seasons, with "recreation," "premier," and "travel" leagues. Travel teams require kids (and their parents) to trek to other towns, often hours away, to play against regional teams from other places. One father I know shuttled his son five hours from Long Island to Cooperstown, New York, to play doubleheaders throughout the spring. Other families have driven to Pennsylvania, Ohio, even Florida, all in the name of fun. It's part of the overscheduling of childhood, the desire to give our children everything, all the time, whenever they want it, and even when they don't.

And yet, despite my cynicism, my own overscheduled life, here I am coaching my son's team during a time of year he should be tossing Wiffle balls in the backyard or the schoolyard rather than taking called balls and strikes from an umpire. It's part of the Dinner with Dad challenge: More time at home means more time to teach my son the two-seam fastball.

"Come on, Simon!" I yell. "Show him the heater!"

Simon looks over at me, nods, pulls his cap down a little lower on his eyes. He's got the look down pat: one part Roger Clemens, two parts Al Hrabosky. He toes the rubber, stares in at the catcher, then fires a pitch that practically knocks the batter back off the plate.

"Strike two!" calls the umpire, himself a kid about thirteen years old.

The other coach rolls his eyes and grits his teeth, but doesn't say anything to the ump. Instead, he shouts encouragement to the hitter, reminding him to bend his knees and keep his elbows back.

The batter has no chance, however, now that the umpire has indicated a strike zone as wide as a cavern. He flails helplessly at the next pitch, which actually hits the dirt before it crosses the plate. Strike three. Game over.

My team runs in from the field, shouting joyfully. They have just won the game in a squeaker, 18–16. They clap Simon on the back, and the grin on his face is enough to melt the coldest heart. In the stands, however, most of the parents look numb. They have endured a three-and-a-half-hour marathon of walks, hit batters, and errors. Little League baseball at its best.

"That was great, Simon," I say when we get into the dugout. And it was. Because despite the walks and wild pitches, he kept his cool even when the calls didn't go his way. He's already progressed a long way from the first games, in which he would collapse on the mound when his teammates made an error or an umpire made a bad call.

"Thanks, Dad," he says. "That last pitch was a ball."

"But you got him to swing," I say. I tell him to grab his equipment because we have to meet his mother.

"Can we go to the diner?" he asks.

"We have to meet Mom first."

"Aw, Dad! I'm hungry!"

I tell him I promised his mother we would go with her to get some flowers from a local landscaper. This is a lie. We are going to the landscaper's, but it's not flowers we are picking up. It's a puppy.

For the next few minutes Simon complains about always having to run errands with his mother—to the point where I'm almost tempted to ruin the surprise, but I don't. The kids have been begging for a dog for at least a year, and though neither Christine nor I are puppy people, we have finally decided to surrender. Christine, in fact, is afraid of dogs, having been bitten on her face when she was a child. I just don't like the way they smell, and I don't care much for their breath, either. But as much as we can't bear the thought of picking up feces, the thought of depriving our children of one of the rites of childhood seems worse. I imagine Simon telling his future spouse that his father was cold and heartless—witness his dislike of puppies—and I decide to eliminate that exhibit from any potential cross-examination.

It's been twenty-six days since I started dining at home, and this week I've had my first failure. On Monday, when I was planning to catch the 5:23, a phone call from a client kept me at work until 6:30. On Tuesday, I made a quick overnight trip to Kansas City, eliminating the possibility of dinner on Wednesday as well. On Friday, a long-scheduled date with my wife kept us out of the house. That left only three days for dinner at home, two short of my goal.

In one week, all the problems that conspire to defeat a man trying to make a simple meal with his family have been made manifest: work, travel, ego. To get home in time means leaving the job at an hour when most people (at least in New York) are still working. To make the money to live as we do means traveling to faraway places (where people don't need as much money to live the same way). To keep my sanity and marriage intact, I must have time to myself and with my wife, away from my children, as much as I love them. The problem, of course, is how to squeeze all these competing concerns within the finite structure of one week—168 hours.

"It's a goal, not a rule," said Christine, when I expressed disappointment at my failure.

"Without rules, how can I have a goal?"

"Don't beat yourself up, Cameron." Like my parents, my wife calls me by my full name when she is trying to make a point, advise, or scold me. "You didn't make it this week; next week you will."

Of course she is right. The point is not to win, as if it's a baseball game, but to set a goal and keep working at it. This week, forces conspired against me. Next week, I will make different choices. Already, I am thinking how I shouldn't have answered the client's call, or promised to call him back later; it was nothing that couldn't wait. As for Kansas, I resolve to limit my socializing to weeks when I am not traveling. Set a course, steer toward it, learn how to say no.

We meet Christine and Lulu in the parking lot. While Christine congratulates Simon on the game, Lulu wants to know where we are going. I sense she suspects something but doesn't really want to be told. Several months ago she caught me slipping money under her pillow when her tooth fell out, and literally sobbed about it all the next morning. "Daddy is the tooth fairy!" she cried, as if I had betrayed her by pretending otherwise.

"We're going to get a shrubbery," I say, making a Monty Python joke, which Simon would normally catch, but in his current state he misses.

"Can't we have dinner first?" Simon asks.

"Shrubbery first. Then dinner."

Christine smiles at me. For the first time, imagining the reaction from our kids, I begin to get excited about the dog. The elaborate ruse; their reluctance to accompany us; the anticipation of the end result. Like throwing a surprise party, the surprise is made more delicious by the subject's utter cluelessness.

We arrive at the landscaper's house, and Simon decides to stay in the car. "Are you sure?" I ask him. "You might want to come out."

"I'm sure," he says sulkily.

We walk up the yard, and the dogs come bounding toward us. Five puppies and their parents, eager to see visitors.

"Oh, Mommy, can we get a puppy?" cries Lulu.

"Okay," says Christine.

"Really?" asks Lulu, as if she can't believe her good fortune.

"Yes," I say. "That's why we're here."

The truth dawns on Lulu, and an enormous smile lights her face. She rushes to the car to tell her brother, and a moment later he comes running toward us, his bad mood vanished, replaced by unabashed joy.

"Which one is ours?" he wants to know.

I point out Sugar, an eight-week-old golden retriever with white highlights on her paws (hence her name, given to her by the landscaper but destined to stick).

Both kids run to Sugar, and she responds by licking their faces, exactly as a puppy should, and before long there are three little creatures rolling around on the ground, frolicking like something out of a Disney movie.

Of course, now that we have a puppy, neither Simon nor Lulu wants to eat. But Christine and I do. We get final instructions from the landscaper and then herd the kids and the dog back to the car. I suggest we go home and quickly boil water for pesto pasta, a staple of Simon's diet since he was three years old, but Christine doesn't want to dirty the kitchen, even with a couple of pots. Plus, she's sick of pesto. Even Simon, I think, is sick of pesto.

But I'm not quite ready to let it go. Since I've only been home for dinner one night so far this week, it seems to me I should at least try to make dinner the next two nights, even if it's something simple and uninventive. Christine says I'm getting caught up again in rules; dinner is dinner, and we're eating together. By that reasoning, I say, we might as well microwave something and sit down in front of the television—as long as we're together, what difference does it make? Cooking is as much a part of dining as eating is, I tell her. Ordering in is losing half the battle.

Christine gives me one of those looks she saves for when my legal training overwhelms my humanity. "The kids just got a puppy," she says. "And I don't want to clean up the kitchen."

I'm not sure the two things are connected, but oddly, I know what she means. In any event, Simon, who hears everything and knows everything, asks if we can order from his favorite restaurant, a place that tries to be all things Asian to all people. In the face of such resistance, I am forced to acknowledge defeat. Since the week has been a bust, I decide to chalk it up to experience and start again on Monday.

We call the restaurant from the car. I order pad thai, Christine orders curried vegetables, Simon orders shu mai and vegetable dumplings, and Lulu orders white rice with steamed tofu. Ordering food reminds me of living in Manhattan, where we filled a drawer with menus and occasionally ordered from two different restaurants if we couldn't agree on the cuisine. In the suburbs, we consider ourselves fortunate that the restaurants stay open until nine.

The puppy sits on the backseat between Simon and Lulu,

basking in their attention, licking their hands and faces. Lulu wants to know if Sugar can eat tofu, and I tell her for now, at least, the puppy needs to eat her own special food. The truth is I don't know much about dogs—though I had one when I was a kid—and both Christine and I share a moment of sober reality. We are suddenly responsible for another mouth to feed, another creature to care for, and though she probably won't go to college or experiment with drugs, raising her will present its own challenges.

We pick up our food, then return to the house, and the kids race around showing the dog everything. She responds by promptly squatting on the family room carpet and urinating.

"Oh, no, Sugar!" I shout, startling her. I look around for something to smack her, but everything is either too heavy or too breakable. By the time I find a magazine, it's too late; she's scurried into the kitchen.

Doors are closed. Rules are imposed. Baking powder is sprinkled on the wet spot. Meanwhile, the food has grown cold, so now we have to nuke it in the microwave. The day is ending very much as it used to end in New York, except our kitchen is bigger and so are our children.

But when we sit down, the puppy curls up at Lulu's feet. Darkness settles outside, and I can actually see the stars. Through an open window, crickets sing their fading song, a lullaby of clean air and green grass, leafy trees and soaring baseballs.

At the table, Simon recounts his victory for his mother. Although she knows very little about the rules of the game, Christine is fascinated by Simon's account, as am I. What he says tells us much more about him than about the actual game. Right now he is saying: I am growing up; I am becoming my own person; listen to the things that are important to me. Christine and I strain to hear every word.

Both kids want to sleep with the puppy, but after the carpet incident, that is out of the question. Besides, we explain, Sugar has her own bed, complete with locking door. Hers locks from the outside, but that is a minor point not worth troubling the children. The books say she will not soil her own space, and we can only hope they're right. Neither of us wants to spill more baking powder.

After the children are asleep, and the dog has been walked two or three times, Christine and I get into bed ourselves.

"Did we make a mistake?" she asks.

"Time will tell," I say.

For some reason, that cracks us up. That two people with an affirmative dislike of dogs should get a puppy seems the height of absurdity, the punch line of a crazy joke. We have both always been impulsive, buying our apartment and then our house without much thought to the price, the neighborhood, the underlying structural soundness. The moment seemed right, and we leaped, much as we had leaped into each other's arms, marriage, children. But we have never missed yet, despite the dizzying distance below and the occasional distance between us.

"Shhh," says Christine. "Did you hear something?"

We both listen intently, but it's only the wind, laughing at us—or with us—time will tell. I fall asleep in my wife's arms and dream I am being tickled by small animals with blond hair and blue eyes who want to know what I am cooking.

The next afternoon Simon and I take the puppy to the local ball field, where Simon attempts to field grounders as Sugar yaps at his feet. Finally we give up, but not before the dog is coated with a fine brown dust, which leads to her first bath in a kiddie pool in the backyard when we get home. The suds spill over onto the patio as Lulu hoses her down, "accidentally" soaking her brother in the process.

The last of the tomatoes have ripened, late this year because of a cool and dry summer. As the kids bathe and dry the dog, I harvest about thirty. Not wanting to waste any, I make a salad generously filled with tomatoes.

"Look at this beauty," I insist at dinner, holding up a small tomato the color of gold.

"Gross," says Lulu.

I can't believe no one loves the tomatoes as much as I do. They are so sweet, their skins popping in my mouth with just the right amount of tartness and sugar. I practically swoon over them, while my family regards me warily as if I were eating snails or tripe. Only Sugar appears interested; she sits by my chair, her fast breath like the bellows of a blacksmith's forge.

I had contemplated making a simple summer pasta with fresh tomatoes and basil, the kind of thing that would be perfect for an Indian summer evening. But not wanting to push my luck, I settle for a much simpler dish: pasta with smothered onions. Because the onions are cooked alone with some butter and olive oil, I can set aside about half the pasta and salt it in a bowl for the kids. They eat contentedly, with no arguments about strange ingredients or unfamiliar tastes, while Christine and I enjoy our meal as well. The onions, cooked for about forty-five minutes over a very low flame, are as sweet as the tomatoes, translucent and candied, more like dessert than dinner.

Fall is upon us, and winter not far behind. The baseball season draws to a close. We gather around the table, food in front of us, a dog at our feet, reminding us that life is full, frantic, and occasionally hyperkinetic.

Puppies, I think, are a lot like children. They will do their business on the floor if you don't watch them closely enough, and will put nearly anything in their mouth. Like children, we overindulge them because they're so cute, and we seem not to learn from our lessons. Bring the dog into the family room, and she will pee on the carpet. Leave her alone for a minute, and she will chew up your shoes. Ditto children.

But it seems to me we can learn a lot from puppies. Like children, they respond to consistency and a firm voice. They love to play, and are happiest when you pay attention. Praise them when they're good, scold them when they're bad (but no hitting!) and keep them on a short leash. Never negotiate.

Of course, we can't lock children in a crate overnight, or leave them in the backyard with a bowl of water. Children also smell a lot better. They rarely drool, and hardly ever chase cars. A puppy, however, will eat nearly anything you place in front of it. Asparagus, broccoli, dirt, very small rocks. A dad can dream of a child with an appetite like a puppy.

I Married a Vegetarian

Chicken stock nearly doomed my marriage.

Christine and I had been dating about two months, still in that phase where the other could do no wrong, where everything was sexy, delicious, intriguing, and there was no such thing as bad breath. I lived in a one-bedroom apartment in Iowa City that occupied the entire ground floor of a three-story house, complete with living room, dining room, porch (with swing), detached garage, and kitchen.* It seemed the gracious thing to do to invite my girlfriend, who lived in the only apartment in Iowa that actually had cockroaches, over to my place for dinner. We were young, in love, and she was a vegetarian.

At first this didn't seem like a serious problem. I rarely ate meat, and Christine occasionally ate fish. She also ate dairy and

---

*For which I paid the exact same amount I would pay to garage my car in New York City several years later.

eggs, which really made her a quasi-vegetarian, while I was a carbo-lover. We could work it out.

But that was before I started stir-frying vegetables and tofu in a soy marinade with chicken stock.

"What's that?" she asked, pointing to the box of bouillon cubes I had set on the counter.

"Bouillon."

"Is it chicken?"

"Not really," I said. "I don't think there's any chicken in it. It's mostly salt."

Christine picked up the box and read the ingredients. "I can't eat this," she said. "It's chicken."

"It's just for the stock."

"There's chicken in it."

"You'll never taste it."

"That's not the point. I'll know it's in there."

"So don't think about it."

"I can't *not* think about it. It's gross."

Christine stood in my kitchen with her hands on her hips, red lips pursed in disgust. I loved this woman and would eventually marry her, but at that moment her refusal not only to eat meat, but to eat a dish prepared with a couple of cubes of flavoring that contained perhaps one micro particle of chicken, struck me as absurd, and I told her so.

Voices were raised, doors slammed, and food left uneaten. By the time calm returned, our relationship had its first scratch, marring its shiny patina, leaving us slightly dented in its wake.

After thirteen years of marriage, however, I had come to a greater appreciation of what it meant to be a vegetarian, and understood that eating a dish prepared with the boiled skin of another creature, no matter how small, might not be palatable. Christine's vegetarianism had little to do with politics and mostly to do with a simple revulsion to eating animals, heightened by the fact that she grew up in a town where her neighbors routinely slaughtered chickens in their backyard, and the sight of bloody headless birds racing around the backyard has stayed with her to this day.*

Thus, I led a kind of dual life: a (quasi) vegetarian at home and a carnivore on the road. When we began to raise our children, I acquiesced to raising them as vegetarians, and although Christine fed the occasional piece of fish to Simon, no other meat crossed his lips for a number of years.

But children will confound you in unexpected ways. At two years old, on New Year's Eve, Lulu grabbed for a piece of filet mignon on my plate. She stuck it in her mouth and chewed with gusto, then reached for another. I can't say I did much to stop her. Secretly, I worried about raising children as vegetarians, and had begun to feel it was unnatural. After all, our teeth and stomachs are biologically and evolutionarily adapted to eat meat. Given how picky our children were, precluding them from eating an entire food group seemed ill advised.

At about the same time, Simon developed a love for hot dogs, which he had sampled at birthday parties and at school. Although Christine felt conflicted about it, she, too, worried about Simon's monomaniacal devotion to macaroni and cheese, and before long, hot dogs appeared in our refrigerator, followed by (organic) chicken nuggets.

These were limited forays, however. For the most part, our family menu remained heavily skewed toward pasta, rice, and other carbohydrates, with cheese, eggs, soybeans, and occasionally

---

* I understood the feeling. After reading *Fast Food Nation*, Eric Schlosser's book on the fast-food industry, I swore I would never eat another hamburger, although I have since gone back on that pledge.

fish providing the protein. Although Christine had softened in her stance against meat, I didn't expect to see any carcasses in our kitchen any time soon.

Thus, imagine my surprise when I come home to find a barbecued chicken on the table, with rice, a fresh salad, and bread. Sunday night, Simon and I have just returned from the movies, and there it is, pretty as you please, sitting on the table. Christine hasn't actually cooked it—she bought it at the supermarket—but it is a carcass, nevertheless, and it is very good.

"What's gotten into you?" I ask.

"I just got tired of the same old, same old."

"But chicken?"

"We've had chicken before."

"No, we haven't."

"Well, turkey."

"That's Thanksgiving. And that's at my parents'."

She shrugs. "I thought you might like it."

Both Lulu and I love it. We devour the chicken, and Lulu asks for the wishbone. Simon is less enthusiastic, although he makes an attempt at a piece, then pushes it around his plate. Christine cooks herself a veggie burger.

When we have finished dinner, the picked-over chicken looks grisly and gelatinous on the serving platter, reminding me that it is, after all, a bird, not unlike the birds that flap around our backyard, just slightly plumper and less coordinated. I try not to think about it too much, and dump the remainder in the trash.

"Shouldn't you save it?" asks Christine.

"For what?"

"I don't know. Chicken soup."

It's an idea, although I can think of plenty of other things I'd rather do than boil a dead bird. In fact, soup seems practically barbarous, unappetizing and slightly nauseating. My reaction makes me wonder if eating meat really is a natural state of affairs, or whether we have evolved beyond it.

Sugar sticks her nose in the garbage, and I shoo her away. She has no qualms about what's for dinner; indeed, in some cultures she would *be* dinner. Why our culture has decided that cows and pigs and chickens are appropriate for eating, but dogs and cats and guinea pigs are not, is a great mystery. To some, lobster is a delicacy; to others, it's a big insect that lives in the water. I love calamari and escargot (which are really just fancy names for squid and snails), but wouldn't touch octopus or eel. Sushi, yes; roe, no. As a child, I loved tongue until I saw one in a delicatessen.

Despite my aversion to certain animal products, however, I doubt I could ever be a vegetarian. I love hamburgers too much, and practically survive on turkey sandwiches. I have managed to keep these illicit cravings from my wife, and to satisfy my urgings outside the home.

The next day, Christine makes a tomato and chickpea casserole. On Thursday, it's tofu and couscous salad. On Friday, she arrives home with a crockpot and announces she is going to make chili.

"Is it something I said?" I ask.

"What do you mean?"

"The sudden flurry of activity in the kitchen."

Not that I'm complaining. In fact, I can't believe my good luck. It's like buy one, get one free. For every meal I make, my wife makes a new one as well.

"It's no fun cooking for one." She explains that when she was just cooking for the kids, her meals tended toward the bland and simple, but now that I am coming home for dinner, she's rediscovered her joy of cooking. "You can't cook without an audience," she says.

I understand what she means: It's hard to be a gourmet when

your audience craves Oreos, Cheetos, and Cheerios. Like a lounge singer trying to perform above the clatter of dishes, cooking for children is often a thankless task, with the emphasis on finishing rather than hitting the high notes. Without an appreciative audience, meals fall upon deaf ears. When Christine and I first started cooking together, we were trying to impress each other, to dazzle with the primal need for nourishment, the same way males and females have always displayed their wares: with bright plumage and hearty roars. We love good food, but we also love the performance, which is why going out to dinner is only partly about the meal and mostly about the service, ambience, and setting.

Saturday morning, Christine sets about chopping fresh cilantro, onions, peppers, and garlic. She stirs dried cumin into the pot. I take Simon and Lulu to the beach, where Sugar gets her first taste of Long Island Sound. The gentle waves lap the shore while she runs into them like playmates. We climb out onto the rocks, and Simon resists my efforts to hold his hand. "I can do it myself, Dad," he says. Of course he can; silly me for even asking. Lulu and I follow at a safe distance, with Sugar on a leash itching to catch up to Simon.

Across the sound we see Long Island, and I can make out the towers of the incinerator at Oyster Bay where, as a kid myself, I used to go to Bar Beach. Back then, our parents had no idea where we were, what we were doing, whom we were with. My mother would open the door and we would be gone, and she would not worry until dinner. Now, as Simon often reminds me, children can't go anywhere without a GPS device strapped to their arm and a cell phone in their pocket. We monitor them like air traffic controllers, orchestrating their every move, negotiating takeoffs and landings. Christine does not let them up the street without phoning our neighbors to make sure they arrive. And forget about riding their bicycles to town; hang-gliding would be less dangerous.

I know they are not really safer—just more accounted for—but once the genie is out of the bottle it will not go back in. No one wants to be the parent who loses a child through inadvertence.

When we are good and cold we bundle back into the car and head to Starbucks. It's the closest Westport has to a café, and though it's not New York City, there is a girl with a tattoo. She listens to an iPod at a corner table. Simon and Lulu order hot chocolates while I get a small coffee.* Lulu slurps hers, leaving whipped cream on her nose, while Simon plunges right in, chugging his down. The kids ask for a cookie, but I draw the line at one sugary treat per visit, which causes a round of negotiation to rival the Kyoto treaty. There are no winners, only compromise, conciliation, and laments. In the end, moderation prevails, however fragile and likely to rupture.

We drive home listening to the soundtrack from *Bring It On,* one of our favorite movies, along with *A Knight's Tale,* both of which use music to tell stories of adversity, courage, and triumph, and the virtue of great clothing. When we get inside, the kids run to Christine, suffering from mommy withdrawal, and even Sugar gets in on the act, wagging her tail, running in circles, and sniffing madly as if hunting for truffles. I retreat to my office and check my e-mail, exhausted by the afternoon. Playing with kids is anything but play; it's hard work, requires constant monitoring, and is not for the faint of heart or weak of imagination. This is why electronic communication is sometimes preferable to the real thing. *To Simon, From Dad: Clean Your Room.*

The metallic smell of cumin seeps under the door, however, and soon lures me back to the kitchen. I leave my e-mail and join Christine. "When's dinner?" I ask.

---

* In Starbucks lingo, a "tall" coffee.

"Chili's almost done," she says. "We're having jasmine rice, and salad."

I realize that I am very hungry. We all are. Lulu and Simon hang around a bowl of chips, grabbing them when Christine's not looking. I take the bowl away from them, and then eat a handful myself. "Hey! No fair!" says Lulu. I give her one, and she asks for five. I offer two, and we settle on three. Simon puts an olive on each finger, then eats them. Lulu wants to try the same trick, but I confiscate the bowl of olives. Then it's on to the salad, from which they pick out the cucumbers and carrots. Finally, just when it seems as if they might snack themselves right out of dinner, Christine serves the chili.

Chili is a dish for the masses, hot and tangy and gooey with cheese. Perfect for a blustery day, or a football game. It gives new meaning to the words "super bowl." It seems that it should also be a dish appreciated by children, since it shares so many common denominators with macaroni and cheese, ketchup, rice and beans. But our children are no normal progeny. They never met a cumin seed they couldn't spit across the room, or a speck of cilantro leaf they couldn't remove from their tongue and place on their napkin as if it were strontium 90.

Lulu refuses to touch the chili. For her, Christine microwaves some cold pasta with butter. "You don't know what you're missing," I say.

"Chili," she says.

It's hard to argue with that kind of logic, so I don't. Instead, I scoop her chili into my bowl and finish both portions. Simon eats half a bowl, despite complaining that it's too spicy, which feels like a small victory. The chili really is quite good, even if the chef and the dish washer are the only ones who think so.

After dinner, I direct the kids to clean up the table with me. This is about as easy as herding cats, and as much fun, but I stay with it because one of the virtues of shared mealtime, I believe, is shared effort. I don't want my children thinking that food just appears magically on the table, then disappears into the disposal. My own father was a virtuoso cleaner, remaining in the kitchen long after everyone else had vanished, scouring microparticles only he could see, humming show tunes to keep himself occupied. Perhaps I've inherited a few of those genes, if not his perfect pitch.

Christine goes upstairs to pack. Tomorrow she's flying to help a close friend move. At the time, the trip seemed an act of generosity—both on her part and mine—but now I'm coming to doubt the wisdom of the decision. I have never cared for both kids for more than a single night, and never while school was in session.

I really question my decision the next morning when I have to wake the kids, pack their lunches, check their backpacks, arrange their playdates, and cover their music lessons, sporting events, and pickups. What was I thinking when I agreed to let her go?

Although Christine has left me a detailed list, the specifics both overwhelm and confuse me. Does Lulu prefer Juicy Juice or Minute Maid? Does Simon get a stainless spoon for his yogurt or will plastic suffice? Can Lulu have a sleepover? Once again I am saddened to discover the breadth of events that occur completely off my radar screen. Little things like what they eat for lunch, or how they order lunch (which, I learn, requires a check to refill a lunch card). Big things like their true feelings about their Spanish teacher (positive) and music teacher (negative). As children we eventually learn that our parents live secret lives, but how many parents consider the unknown lives of their children? Even the mother (or father) who puts them on the bus every morning may be ignorant as to what really goes on in the classroom and schoolyard. The father who rarely sees them every day not only doesn't know what they are doing, but doesn't even know what he doesn't know.

When I think of the time I waste responding to e-mail, surfing the Internet, blabbing on my cell phone, and socializing with colleagues, it fills me with deep remorse, as if all the time were piling up on my shoulders, knocking me on the back of my head, saying to me, "Hey, idiot, what were you thinking?"

After school I take them grocery shopping, and we buy Gatorade, Pop-Tarts, Chips Ahoy, Ben & Jerry's ice cream, ground beef, frozen sausages, Wheat Thins, and radishes—things my wife never buys. They scamper down the aisles, pulling coupons from the dispensers that hang low from the shelves. They fight for position on the shopping cart, pushing each other aside and clambering to the front. We reach the "seasonal" aisle, and Simon wants a plastic pumpkin, a Halloween mask, a sled. I let them race down the comic book aisle, where they read Archie comics until I circle back around, the cart loaded with treats.

"Can I buy this?" asks Simon, by which he means, will you buy me an *Archie*. I agree, because I'm a sucker for anything printed, even though I know he will read it in three minutes in the back of the car. Lulu wants *Betty & Veronica*, and soon I'm six dollars poorer.

When we return home, I get busy in the kitchen, making pasta with a simple red sauce. Neither kid will eat it, however, and I'm forced to rinse off the sauce, re-strain the pasta, and melt some butter for both. I try not to be disappointed, telling myself that they're tired and miss their mother, and it's only red sauce, after all. After dinner Simon and I sit down to do his math homework, and I have my first taste of my own eventual inconsequence. As best I can tell, the problem calls for the application of differential calculus, which I nearly failed in college. After trying to solve for x in twelve different ways, Simon shows me how to do it—a simple trial-and-error strategy that seems designed to encourage blind guessing. When I criticize his math instruction, however, he points out that he solved the problem. It's hard to argue with results, so I don't.

Instead, we watch a DVD, and the kids gobble popcorn. At least, I tell myself, corn is a vegetable.

The next night, after an unusually warm day, I barbecue some chicken. Although Simon picks at a few pieces, Lulu refuses to eat anything because she can taste the lemon marinade I've foolishly used. This time, I lose my temper, and send her upstairs without supper, but I relent and give her a yogurt when her howls threaten to peel paint from the walls.

By the third night, I am exhausted, cranky, and tired of cooking. All I want is for my wife to come home. I plan on taking the kids to the diner, but at the last minute inspiration strikes. In the refrigerator is a tub of cold rice, left over from one of Christine's meals. I decide to make fried rice, a dish I loved as a child and, I assume, a sure winner.

I stir-fry some of our favorite vegetables, things that I know the kids will eat: sugar snap peas, carrots, celery, bean sprouts. To this I add a mixture of soy sauce, garlic, sesame oil, sweet cooking wine, and rice vinegar, then thicken the sauce with cornstarch. I set the vegetables aside and go to work on the rice. The trick here is to use plenty of oil—preferably something heavy like peanut oil. When the wok is good and hot, I crack an egg directly into the oil, scramble it, then add the rice. After a few minutes of cooking, I add the vegetables and soy sauce. Soon, I have some pretty authentic-looking fried rice. Better yet, it tastes just as good as it looks. I congratulate myself on a meal well made.

My kids, however, have a different opinion. The vegetables are cooked, they complain. It does no good to point out that cooking them in a wok makes them hot outside, crunchy inside—which is the point of using a wok. There are tears, and whines, and cries, and the kids don't react too well, either. This time, I do send them to bed without dinner. Then, in a snit, I toss the rice into the trash and stomp around the kitchen, sending Sugar scurrying out of my way. I am Mad Dad, scorned by the very mouths he has tried to feed. Three times I have tried to make something they will enjoy, and three times I have struck out. It's enough to send a man back to the office, or to cooking school.

I can hear the kids upstairs complaining that they're hungry, but eventually they stop and all is silent except for the sound of the dog sniffing for morsels I have missed. My fury spent, I sit in the darkened family room, shades drawn as if in mourning. I realize this is a version of what my wife has endured for years: single parenting, tone-deaf audience, unpalatable choices. In that environment, cooking skills wither and die, until there is nothing left but plain pasta with butter. It's enough to make a parent reach for the microwave—and stick his head inside.

As I reach the depths of self-pity, the lock clicks, and my wife walks in the door. Let's just say I have never been more appreciative, or hungrier.

On the Internet, No One Knows You're a Dad

We are creatures of habit. Most of us eat the same thing every day for breakfast (in my case, half a peanut butter sandwich or yogurt with granola) and the same thing for lunch (turkey sandwich). We snack on the same favorite foods (salted peanuts), crave the same sweets (peanut M&M's), enjoy the same beverages (coffee and caffeine-free Diet Coke), and order the same cocktails (scotch on the rocks).

When it comes to dinner, however, we crave variety. Habit gives way to desire, repetition to novelty. It may be fine to eat the same peanut butter sandwich for breakfast ten days in a row, but anyone who ate spaghetti with meatballs for more than a couple days suffers from OCD or a serious financial handicap. In graduate school, living on a dime, I would occasionally make a lasagna last for several days. Near the end of its useful life, however, I would rather eat my shoe than another noodle. I nearly ruined myself for pizza and bagels by subsisting on them for nearly a year after law school. During her pregnancy, my wife was commanded by her obstetrician to eat Häagen-Dazs ice cream, and to this day she can no longer stomach it.*

Yet children seem to thrive on repetition. My son could eat pesto three meals a day (and has). My daughter could eat plain pasta until she keeled over from anemia. Both of them could probably have pizza every single night for dinner without complaint. Conversely, they view new food with fear and loathing. Shrimp is a dreaded adversary. Broccoli and cauliflower rank directly below homework on the torture scale (and just above bathing). Sometimes their likes and dislikes have a weird sort of logic; other times, as in my daughter's refusal to eat certain shaped pasta (elbow, butterfly), it seems just plain weird.

Of course, adults are not immune from food quirks. My wife enjoys salsa, tomato sauce, and ketchup, but loathes tomatoes (and corn and raw onions). My sister eats beef but hates chicken and fish. A friend will eat sushi but not lox or salmon. Go figure.

There's some research indicating that picky eating has a biological basis. In particular, children appear to have an evolutionary preference for bland food because of the risk of toxins found in more distinctive-tasting foods. This may even explain their preference for repetition: Once they know something won't kill them, they prefer to eat it again and again. They also have a predisposed aversion to fruits and vegetables, which scientists believe evolved to protect them from eating poisonous berries and leaves. Children begin showing these food preferences around age two (which is when they would be weaned in traditional societies), and they grow strongest between the ages of four and eight. New foods are most likely to be accepted between ages two and four. After that,

---

*We are all familiar with the urban myth of the boy whose parents cured him of smoking by forcing him to smoke two packs of cigarettes, one after another, until, sickened by nicotine, he swore off the deadly habit.

it can take ten to twelve tries to introduce a child to a new food (if at all). Children also have a different sense of taste than adults, preferring sweet, salty, and sour-tasting foods. In one study, for example, children aged five to nine were shown to prefer concentrated citric acid such as that found in Sour Patch Kids candy. Tastes may also be influenced by what a baby's mother eats while pregnant and while breast-feeding. Another study found that the children of mothers who drank carrot juice daily during pregnancy preferred carrot-flavored cereal, in contrast to children whose mothers didn't drink carrot juice.*

Even Darwin, frustrated by his children's tastes, was moved to write:

> I will add that formerly it looked to me as if the sense of taste, at least with my own children when they were still very young, was different from the adult sense of taste; this shows itself by the fact that they did not refuse rhubarb with some sugar and milk which is for us an abominable disgusting mixture and by the fact that they strongly preferred the most sour and tart fruits, as for instance unripe gooseberries and Holz apples.[†]

Sometimes, however, I can't help believing picky eating is just about control. This is why anorexics refrain and bulimics purge. Particularly for children, food is a way to exercise some authority over an environment (the home) and people (parents) against

---

* This would explain children's aversion to bitter foods, because mothers are highly sensitive to bitter foods during their pregnancy and usually refrain from eating acid-tasting foods such as vegetables.

† Charles Darwin, "Biographische Skizze eines Kleinen Kindes." *Kosmos,* 367–76 (1877).

whom they are mostly powerless. Although hard data are difficult to come by, anecdotal evidence suggests that children have become pickier, that in our desire to please, to be all things to all children, we have allowed them to gain the upper hand. It is a cliché, but also true, that when we were young we were not presented with as many choices at the dinner table. My mother never prepared a separate meal for the kids, and if we didn't like Brussels sprouts or liver with onions, we were out of luck. Now, we have friends who come for dinner and bring their own pasta for their children. When we travel to my parents' we are never without at least one box of Annie's macaroni and cheese for Simon. When my daughter refuses to eat what she has been served, we scour the refrigerator for an alternative. In short, I am convinced my children "play" me just as a puppeteer plays a marionette.

But knowing it and living it are two different things. While I don't want to capitulate to my children's food quirks, I also don't want to make food a battleground. Tomorrow's anorexics are today's fighters over pasta shapes. No child has died from eating too much macaroni, our pediatrician told us. Their tastes will diversify; they are not born loving Brussels sprouts. Offer them healthful meals, and help them make healthy choices. Do not force-feed.

This seems like good advice when Christine is cooking, but annoyingly simplistic after Lulu refuses to eat pasta with tomato sauce and artichokes, one of my favorite recipes from *The New Basics* cookbook, even after I remove the artichokes.

"I hate artichokes!" she screams.

"You've never had an artichoke!" I scream back.

"I don't care!"

Eventually, Christine calms us down, and we finish our dinner in a state of détente, if not peace.

"I don't understand," I say later, when the kids are asleep. "She didn't even taste the sauce."

"She doesn't like artichokes," says Christine.

"That's ridiculous."

We are cleaning up the kitchen together, something we have been doing with more regularity these days. Until recently I never cleaned the kitchen and can't remember the last time I unloaded the dishwasher. As for the laundry, I haven't touched it since New York. For four years, Christine has been cooking, cleaning, shopping, washing, drying, folding, straightening, vacuuming, carpooling, making lunches, checking homework, filling out permission slips, camp forms, and medical questionnaires, returning phone calls, securing babysitters, making playdates, and keeping our social calendar. It has gotten to the point where I actually don't know where all the kitchen utensils are stored or where my daughter's clothes go. When I need a garlic press, I yell for Christine, and feel aggrieved until she answers me, as if it's her fault that it's not kept next to the knife sharpener and the carrot peeler.

"How can she know what she likes, if she doesn't try it?" I ask.

"It's a lot to ask a six-year-old to eat an artichoke."

"I didn't ask. I took it out."

"Maybe you could disguise it next time."

"Paint a mustache on it?"

She laughs, and I am struck again by the oddities of food preferences. Once, in Norway, I ate whale blubber, which was so heavily drowned in a brown sauce that it was impossible to discern its taste. In Czechoslovakia I ate kidneys because I couldn't understand a word on the menu. I've eaten intestines in Chinatown and pituitary glands in midtown, both masquerading under euphemistic names. Maybe that's the secret: Camouflage everything in indistinguishable sauces and indecipherable languages.

"Well, she's got to eat something other than plain pasta all the time," I conclude.

"She will." Christine hands me a stainless-steel sauté pan, a wedding gift, which I dry and place in a cabinet beneath the counter. She reminds me that Simon was the same way: adventurous until he turned six, then eating nothing with color. It is only recently that he has begun to emerge from his self-imposed albino food phase. Better, stronger, faster. Like the Six Million Dollar Man, but only half as expensive.

The next day, leaving nothing to chance, I go to Barnes & Noble and spend an hour perusing the cookbook section. There, I discover I am not alone. In my corner, helping me plan delicious, nutritious, and, most important, speedy meals is Rachael Ray of Food Network fame, whose books include *30-Minute Meals, 30-Minute Meals 2,* and, of course, *30-Minute Meals for Kids.* Joining her on the shelf are *30-Minute Meals for Dummies, Biggest Book of 30-Minute Meals, 150 Tasty Recipes in 30 Minutes or Less, Mouthwatering Meals in Under 30 Minutes, Wholesome Family Recipes in 30 Minutes or Less, Pillsbury 30-Minute Meals, 4 Ingredient Recipes for 30 Minute Meals, Letting Your Microwave Work for You (in 30 Minutes or Less), 30 Low-Fat Vegetarian Meals in 30 Minutes or Less, From Bangkok to Bali in 30 Minutes, 30-Minute Recipes from an Italian Kitchen,* and *30 Minute Cooking* (both an Indian and a vegetarian version). If a half-hour is too long to be tied down in the kitchen, there's *The Complete Idiot's Guide to 20-Minute Meals, Cooking to Beat the Clock: Inspired Meals in 15 Minutes, The Working Parents Cookbook,* which promises meals in 15 to 30 minutes, and even *The Weeknight Survival Cookbook: How to Make Healthy Meals in 10 Minutes.* For slowpokes, there's *Every Night Italian: 120 Simple, Delicious Recipes You Can Make in 45 Minutes or Less* and *The New York Times 60-Minute Gourmet.*

The cookbooks all promise no-muss, no-fuss meals that my

family will adore. Although I am dubious, I purchase *Kid Food: Rachael Ray's Top 30 30-Minute Meals.* It's a small hardcover book resembling a child's sketch pad, complete with spiral binding and food photos in bright primary colors, dedicated to "picky eaters everywhere," with recipes like "Dilly of a Quesadilla" and "Meatza Pizza Burgers." Here, I reason, I can at least find the inspiration that will help me triumph over my children's food irrationalities.

When I get home I spend another couple hours surfing the Internet, where information about food, cooking, and recipes ranges from the slick commercialism of the Food Network to clubmom.com, where moms from around the world can join and share recipes. There are websites for "busy people," "busy cooks," "easy cooking," "minute meals," "time-saving entrées," and "quick and easy meals," as well as sites for moms who don't cook, busy working moms, vegetarian moms, vegan moms, lactose-intolerant moms, carnivorous moms, and moms who would prefer to be in St. Croix but have to put another pot on the burner. There aren't too many sites for busy working dads who are trying to get home to make dinner, but there are a few blogs where single dads tout their diaper-changing prowess. My favorite website is CookingByNumbers.com, where you can check off the ingredients you have in your kitchen, and it will detail the recipes you can make with them. I select "chocolate" and "onions," and sure enough, I get a recipe for "chocolate dream" (which, unfortunately, does not use the onion). It's not something I'd make for dinner—at least not yet—but I print out the recipe, along with several others.

There's also an e-mail from a local chef who's started a company that offers "cooking classes for busy moms." She's read an article I've written in *The Wall Street Journal* about dining with my kids and suggests I attend her class, which, conveniently, meets ten minutes from my house. I go there one evening and watch her prepare four delicious and tasty meals in exactly one hour—fifteen minutes each, as promised. Her tips include buying frozen squares of garlic and basil that are available at Trader Joe's, precooked bags of rice that just need to be microwaved, premixed spices like "Italian seasoning" and "Greek seasoning," and premixed frozen vegetables like roasted corn and red peppers. She uses lots of shrimp—which she tells her children is "pink chicken"—and easy meats to cook in a pan, like sausage and lamb chops. For vegetarians, she tells me to substitute vegetarian sausage or extra-firm tofu. I leave feeling inspired, hopeful, and sated with good food.

But when I make two of her meals for my children—cassoulet and garlic shrimp—they hate them. It doesn't matter what I call the shrimp, Lulu recognizes seafood when she sees it. As for the cassoulet, although I call it "franks and beans," neither of my kids likes chunks of sausage, while my vegetarian wife thinks I'm being passive-aggressive. This is the problem, I think, with so much cooking for children: It's devised by adults with adults in mind. One of the chef's recipes calls for scallops, which few adults I know, let alone children, enjoy. Another calls for coconut milk, which my kids wouldn't touch even if it were the only thing to drink on a deserted island. Rachael Ray's cookbook includes foods like eggplant, which my kids can't stand. Another recipe I get from the Internet for salmon claims, "It's delicious, easy to find and easy to cook, and almost everybody likes it." Is she kidding? My kids hate salmon, as do most of the children I know. I wonder if this expert has any children of her own.

I need something basic, normal, kid-friendly, proven, reliable, and vegetarian. I need macaroni and cheese. The real kind, not the meal in the box. Comfort food that I know I can depend upon. Cheesy goodness for the masses.

On the Internet there are literally thousands of recipes for mac 'n' cheese—from designer versions with blue cheese and crème fraîche to basic Velveeta. I select one that calls for penne and cheddar cheese, and boil water for DeCecco penne, my favorite.

Outside, the trees have given up their tenuous hold on their leaves, which now sit in several large piles awaiting pickup on the lawn. The kids dive into them, shouting and shoving, while Sugar runs around them barking encouragement. When they see me, they perform a couple of tricks for my benefit, somersaulting into the leaves like gymnasts.

"Be careful," I say, which always struck me as a ridiculous warning when issued by my own parents (right up there with "drive carefully"), as if children will pay any attention or change their behavior accordingly. Yet here I am, mimicking them, in more ways than one. It's true that we become our parents, appreciating their idiosyncrasies even as we develop a few new ones of our own.

"What's for dinner, Dad?" asks Lulu.

"Macaroni and cheese," I say.

"All right!" says Simon.

"Arrrgggghh," says Lulu.

"You'll like it," I promise.

"I won't!" she says.

I ignore her and return to the kitchen, where I finish boiling the pasta until it is al dente. I drain and set aside, then sauté a small onion with two tablespoons of butter until translucent. I add two tablespoons flour, one teaspoon salt, one teaspoon Dijon mustard, and some pepper, stir well, then turn up the heat and add two cups of milk. As the milk thickens, I grease a 9 x 6 baking dish and fill it with the pasta. Then I combine three cups of cheddar cheese with the milk and pour the mixture over the pasta, top it with one cup of breadcrumbs, and set it in the oven to bake at 350.

While the macaroni is baking, I chop some iceberg lettuce and red cabbage for a salad. The nutritional value of the cabbage will counteract the worthlessness of the iceberg lettuce, I reason. Tossing some rolls in the oven with the macaroni, I set the table, fill the glasses, and call the kids for dinner. This is more complicated than I expect because first the dog comes but the kids do not, then the kids come but the dog does not. We run around the front yard trying to corral Sugar into the house until, exhausted, she finally acquiesces.

Banging into the kitchen, the kids run to the table, while Christine emerges from her office and gives me a quick peck.

"Mmm. Macaroni." She approves. It reminds her of Idaho dinners: meatloaf, Hamburger Helper, milk noodles. All the things we loved as kids, then rarely get to eat anymore until we have kids ourselves.

I carry the pan to the table and set it on the trivets we received as a housewarming gift when we first moved to New York. I no longer remember the giver, but the trivets have done their duty for thirteen years, protecting us from searing and scorching, holding our pans, and keeping our food on the table. If only everything else held up as well.

The macaroni looks perfect. Browned on top, sizzling with cheese, crunchy and chewy. The platonic ideal of macaroni. The poster child for baked pasta products.

The kids, however, refuse to touch it.

"It's macaroni and cheese!" I thunder. "You've eaten it a hundred times!"

But, no, they haven't. They've eaten Annie's a hundred times, which is as different from what I've just cooked as foie gras.

"It's burnt," complains Lulu.

Christine explains that the browned surface is just breadcrumbs, considered a delicacy in certain households. The crunchy noodles are what happens to pasta when it's been baked for twenty minutes, exactly as the recipe required. The chewy cheese is orange, not white, simply because it contains a food coloring, but it is, in substance, no different from the white cheese they are used to consuming.

"I hate it!" wails Lulu.

Simon is a bit more circumspect, but he, too, rebuffs my pleas. He tries the tiniest bite, then proclaims himself dissatisfied. "It's burnt, Dad," he says, echoing Lulu, as if it were the most obvious thing in the world.

"It's not burnt!" I can barely contain myself. In two seconds I go from happy-go-lucky dad to trigger-happy dad, a thin wire tripping my switch. I am outraged that after all the effort I have put into dinner—the thinking, the planning, the shopping, the cooking—these ungrateful wretches could be so . . . ungrateful. How dare they not appreciate what I, their father, have worked so hard to achieve.

Christine acts as peacemaker again, stepping between us and offering to find something palatable for the kids in the refrigerator. This makes things worse, as far as I am concerned. I tell her there's nothing wrong with the macaroni, and that we are just empowering our children to order us around. Today, macaroni; tomorrow, shoplifting and drugs. Pick your battles, she says to me, and don't make an issue out of a molehill. "They've never had macaroni with breadcrumbs," she explains. "It's a new thing."

"They've had bread! They've had crumbs! They can have breadcrumbs!"

"You're behaving like a tyrant."

I blow smoke rings through my nose and fire from my throat, then stomp upstairs to the privacy of the master bathroom where I slowly simmer until the steam escaping from my ears dissipates.

I need help. I am willing to admit it. I am defeating the very purpose of making dinner with my family by turning mealtime into a conflict and creating memories of moping rather than doting. How soon before my children prefer dinner without Dad to dinner with Dad? How soon before they hide when they hear me cooking? It's just macaroni and cheese, I tell myself; it's not cocaine or guns or drag racing, any number of potential thrills experienced by parents courtesy of their children. Have some perspective; take a chill pill; calm down.

I splash cold water on my face, and as I do there's a knock at the door. It's Lulu.

"I'm sorry I didn't eat your macaroni," she says, her eyes downcast, hair covering her mouth.

I know she's been sent here by her mother, and in that moment I feel like the ogre I have been. It's enough to make tears come to my eyes, though I wipe them quickly away. My children shouldn't have to come upstairs to bring me back to the table. Even if they have played me like a tuba, I should know better than to react as I have. This is what it means to be a parent: to do as I do, to lead by example, not to run upstairs and lock myself in the bedroom like a teenager.

I scoop Lulu into my arms, feeling her stomach cushion my rib cage. "I'm sorry," I whisper.

"I don't like macaroni and cheese," she says.

"I know you don't. That's okay."

"Why couldn't you make something else?"

"What would you like?"

"I don't know."

She snuggles closer against me, her feet pressing into my belt. I realize this is probably the last year I can carry Lulu. Simon is already too heavy and too tall. It was just yesterday that she could fit in the length of one arm, her head cradled in the palm of my hand, her feet extending to my biceps. I remember bringing her home from the hospital, this miracle, this second child, already so different from our first in her tranquillity, her sleepy limbs, her wide-spaced almond eyes. Every dad wants a daughter, just as every dad wants a son. How lucky am I to have two beautiful children, one of each, headstrong, humorous, and hungry. Their wish is my command.

"We'll figure it out," I promise.

Then we head back downstairs for the kitchen.

Pot Luck, Pasta, and Potatoes

I have a dream. In it, I live in a college town somewhere in New England or the Midwest that vaguely resembles Ann Arbor. My house is a rambling Victorian with five bedrooms, lots of nooks and crannies, and a porch. I wake up early, make coffee, and spend an hour or two writing before waking the kids and my wife. I help get them ready for school, and after they're gone, I head to my job at the local university, a job which consists of teaching writing or law but is not exceptionally taxing, and the students I teach are bright and hungry to learn. I attend a couple of meetings, read for a while, go to lunch with colleagues, and when I return I write for a few more hours.

Then it's time to start thinking about dinner. Fortunately, we have a great food co-op in this dream town of mine. I peruse the aisles, deciding which delicious and nutritious bulk food item will make the beginnings of a great dinner. I buy what I need and return to my eclectic but structurally sound house, which is quiet and empty because my wife has taken the kids to music lessons or soccer practice. Setting aside the groceries, I start my dinner preparations. Then, while things simmer, or settle, or rise, I put on my exercise clothes (it is always about sixty-five degrees in this town, with low humidity), and go for an easy five-mile run through the streets, where I see college and graduate students out on the lawns of their own rambling Victorians, playing Frisbee, listening to music, and doing the things that students do when someone else is making dinner for them. Some of them wave because they recognize me; others just appreciate the sight of a middle-aged professor doing his best to fight advancing decrepitude.

When I get home, there is a message on the answering machine from my brother, who says he's flying out next weekend for a conference at the medical school and is looking forward to staying with us for a couple of days. My wife and kids are home now, and they come downstairs to ask what I am cooking. Although it's something they've never had before, they are excited to try it and ask if they can help me prepare it. I give them each a task, and while my wife makes a salad (from vegetables grown in our own backyard, of course), we finish making dinner.

We sit down to eat at the same time, and no one has to be pulled away from the television or the computer. The food is delicious, warm, and spicy, and everyone has seconds. Conversation is lively, and my daughter does some dead-on impressions of famous singers. My son tells us about a book report he is writing. When we are finished eating, everyone helps clear the table, and then while my wife gives our daughter a bath, I help my son with his math.

The kids brush their teeth and go to bed without protest. My son stays up an extra fifteen minutes reading a book by C. S. Lewis. He shuts off his own lights. My wife and I go downstairs and watch an episode of *Curb Your Enthusiasm* that we have rented on DVD. Afterwards, we go to bed, and my wife massages my back before we fade to black. . . .

In reality, I am on the train again, making my two-hour commute. Mornings are palatable, enjoyable even, as I get to read and write in the uninterrupted solitude of a train ride.* Evenings are much worse: I'm hungry, tired, and aching to get home. I spend four hours a day commuting, I realize, which is twenty hours every five-day workweek, one thousand hours a year (with two weeks for vacation), forty thousand hours over a forty-year career. That's one thousand six hundred sixty-six days and nights spent commuting, or about four years spent entirely on a train and subway. Allowing eight hours for sleep, it's more like six years on a train, alone, isolated, separated from my family.

Of course, I am not alone. According to the U.S. Census Bureau, more than 2.8 million people have "extreme commutes"—more than 90 minutes in one direction.† Meanwhile, the length of the average commute grew by 13 percent between 1990 and 2000, and 7.6 percent of commuters traveled more than an hour to work (up from 6.0 percent in 1990). New York had the highest average commute time of any major metropolitan area—38.3 minutes—and also the most workers with "extreme commutes." Lengthy commutes create job dissatisfaction, according to many experts, while the gains are hardly worth it. An article in *Business Week* magazine notes, "People usually overestimate the value of the things they'll obtain by commuting—more money, more material

---

Except, of course, when the trains are delayed or missing cars because of mechanical problems, or when my seatmate insists on talking on his cell phone to his broker during the entire ride.

On average, Americans spent 100 hours a year commuting, which was longer than most people get for vacation (80 hours). The average daily commute to work lasted 24.3 minutes in 2003. Connecticut residents actually had a shorter commute than average—23.6 minutes.

goods, more prestige—and underestimate the benefit of what they are losing: social connections, hobbies, and health."

Among my friends and colleagues, my commute is bad, but not the worst. Many Westport residents travel to Wall Street, at the southern tip of Manhattan. One of my law school colleagues commutes from New Haven, and another one comes in from northwestern Connecticut, trips that take at least thirty minutes more than mine. We do it for the kids, our spouses, the schools, the backyard, clean air, fresh water, the golden life.

But there are some things I can change, and I set about to change them. For one thing, my regular trips to Kansas City are mostly a thing of the past. For another, I've cut my commute to three days a week, working the other two days at home (when Christine permits it) or the library and Starbucks (when she does not). I am fortunate to be on an academic schedule, with limited teaching responsibilities, and equally fortunate to have a skill (lawyering) that I can ply almost anywhere. I am not a bestselling novelist, but so far, with one exception, I have managed to get home for dinner as planned.

Here's my typical week:

Monday: Catch 6:46 A.M. train. Work in New York. Leave school by 4:50 P.M. to catch 5:23 home. Arrive home at 6:35, in time for dinner.

Tuesday: Catch 6:46 A.M. train. Work in New York. Teach evening class. Leave school by 9:50 P.M. to catch 10:22 home. Arrive home at 11:35. Ouch.

Wednesday: Work at home. Cook dinner.

Thursday: Catch 6:31 A.M. train. Work in New York. Leave school by 4:15 P.M. to catch 4:49 home. Arrive home at 6:00 in time for dinner.

Friday: Work at home. Cook dinner.

This is not impossible, and even allows me one "free" weekend night, as long as there are no emergencies, no unplanned late nights, no unscheduled meetings, no trips to Kansas, no breakdowns or delays on Metro-North. Of course, I often find myself working late into the night, after the kids have gone to sleep, but at least I am home.

I get into a groove. In my search to find things my kids will eat I make shrimp with olives and capers, egg rolls and Chinese noodles, fried chicken and asparagus, shrimp with red peppers and rice. I come home to an empty cupboard and make one of my favorite meals: pot luck. This involves cooking dinner with whatever happens to be in the refrigerator and pantry: an ancient carrot, anchovies, half a carton of orange juice, a chocolate bar, yogurt. Years ago *The New York Times* had famous chefs follow random New Yorkers back to their apartments, where they did the same.* The meals they cooked up with just a package of ramen noodles and a bruised banana were awe-inspiring. Best of all, they were cheap, if not free, relying entirely on ingredients often forgotten by the homeowner. The potluck challenge fuels my pioneer spirit. We are not exactly eating our horses, but it satisfies the primordial urge to nourish, even when the provisions leave something to be desired. So I cook spicy peanut noodles (with half a jar of peanut butter and some sesame oil) and falafel (from a mix) with pita. I make breakfast for dinner, one of my favorite things to eat, harkening back to college days and 2 A.M. trips to the all-night diner.

* In 1995, the Food Network debuted a show called *Ready, Set, Cook!* which gave two teams ten dollars to buy ingredients and twenty minutes to make a meal using those ingredients. Recently, the Discovery Channel broadcast a show called *Go Ahead, Make My Dinner,* in which two chefs faced off against each other with limited ingredients and time to make as many delicious meals and desserts as possible.

The kids, however, continue to eat very little of what I cook. Simon loves Chinese noodles and will eat a shrimp or two, and Lulu likes fried chicken, although the second time, when I make it without the batter—just floured and fried in oil—she complains bitterly. Mostly, my meals fall on insipid palates. My biggest fan is my wife, who gobbles nearly everything with abandon (except chicken), noting that I am going to ruin her waistline. At five seven and 125 pounds, I tell her she can afford it.

Emboldened, I embark on new culinary adventures. A colleague suggests I try making my own pasta. This strikes me as a perfect meal, something I used to love in the late '80s when fresh pasta was all the rage and I would invite dates back to my law school apartment for dinner, impressing them with my culinary savoir faire. But to make it myself I need a machine, special utensils, an Italian grandmother. My colleague (who is Italian) reassures me that no such accoutrements are required, just kids and an appetite.

I gather mine in the kitchen and announce the plan. I will mix and knead, Simon will roll, and Lulu will cut. Though they are resistant at first, they soon see the appeal of playing with food as a form of cheap entertainment. We measure out two cups of flour and combine it with two eggs, a little salt, and some water. No real kneading is necessary, just some firm mixing, until the dough has a rubbery consistency—neither too moist nor too dry. Simon pounds away with the rolling pin, until I help him press down and push forward. His forearms strain with the effort, but he remains intent on doing it himself and I help him as little as possible. When we have a relatively flat oblong pancake, Lulu and I take the pizza cutter and run it the length of the dough, slicing flat noodles and laying them onto a cookie sheet sprinkled with flour. We boil some water, and while the kids spread flour around the kitchen and themselves, I make a quick spinach salad.

There is a moment, when you're cooking something you've never made before, that feels like stepping to the edge of a cliff. You're either going to fall to your death, or soar away on the wings of a transcendent experience. I feel that way as I add the pasta to the boiling water. Either it will lump together like a gooey mess, or boldly take us where we have never gone before. Time, and chemistry, will tell.

Slowly I watch the dough settle into the pot, not daring to touch it. Then I gently stir with a pasta spoon. Miraculously, the pasta comes unstuck and separates into floating tendrils, each one made by hand. Like sand turning into computer chips, or dinosaurs into oil, the transformation of ordinary matter into precious material transfixes me. I made that, I think. *We made that.* I call Simon and Lulu over to gaze in amazement with me, but by this point they have wandered off to the family room to watch SpongeBob, a trail of white powder my only clue as to their whereabouts.

With no time to waste, I whip up a quick tomato sauce which consists of nothing more than crushed tomatoes, garlic, oregano, basil, marjoram, and salt. Not one for the record books, but I have only six minutes. The real investment here is the pasta; everything else is just a side dish.

The timer rings. The pasta is ready. I pour it into a colander, shake, and sprinkle with salt. I call the family for dinner, and this time the kids come running, anxious to see what has become of our experiment. The noodles jiggle like something electric, curled and fat in their bed. I ladle them out carefully to everyone.

There's fresh Parmesan cheese, fresh bread, and my spinach salad. Lulu declines sauce, but Simon accepts a little.

I try not to observe too closely, but it's impossible not to hold my breath as my daughter picks up the first noodle and sucks it into her mouth. She chews carefully, thoughtfully, then says, "Dad, do you have any salt?"

This is a good sign. The mere fact she is willing to enhance her meal with food additives suggests a willingness to compromise. Of course, we will soon have to deal with her overconsumption of sodium, but that's another story.

She takes a bite, and then another bite. I am not watching. Instead, to distract her, I ask everyone at the table what they did today.

"Sugar and I flew to the moon," says Christine.

"Really?" asks Lulu.

"No," says Christine. "Really it was Mars."

"*Mah*-ahm," says Lulu.

This leads to the invention of a game Christine calls "Is it true?" It consists of going around the table and reporting two things—one of which happened, one which did not. Simon starts.

"Today I had orchestra practice," he says. "Today I played football."

"Football!" says Lulu, who knows that Simon plays every day at recess, unless there's a tornado or a plague of locusts.

"Yes!" says Simon, a game-show host.

Christine's turn. "Today I went shopping at Anthropologie," she says. "Today I made mobiles for Simon's Art Smart class."

"Art Smart!" says Simon.

"Correct," says Christine. "Lulu?"

Lulu inhales an entire noodle, the end whipping against her lip. I try not to smile.

"Today I had music. Today I went to the beach."

"Music!" everyone guesses, because we know that although Lulu often dreams of the beach, we live at the wrong latitude.

"Yes," says Lulu, disappointed.

"Cam?" asks Christine.

"Today I made mud pies," I say. "Today I made fresh pasta."

"Pasta!" say Lulu and Simon together.

"Can I have some more?" asks Lulu.

"Me, too," says Simon.

I'm a sucker for sentimental movies. The national anthem brings a lump to my throat. I save old birthday cards and love letters in a secret drawer of my desk. Maybe this explains why, as I scoop out some more noodles for my children, I feel like crying.

It's been forty-seven days since I started coming home for dinner (but who's counting?), and I can feel slow improvement. We have moved from blanket rejection to grudging, albeit sporadic, acceptance; from disgust and disinterest to mere disinclination. That's progress.

After my success with the pasta, I get Simon to eat guacamole with the burritos I make the following night, and Lulu discovers she loves cilantro. The kids may not crave fancy dishes, but they are not entirely without hope. Neither am I.

Sunday morning I wake early. The house is quiet and warm. Sugar licks me until I distract her with food and water. I brew coffee, then rummage through the refrigerator for breakfast. There are cold potatoes, eggs, and frozen veggie sausages. Lulu loves home fries, I know, so I set to chopping the potatoes and a small onion. By the time she stumbles downstairs, eyes bleary with sleep, the big cast-iron skillet is sizzling. She asks what I am making, but instead of answering I lift her in my arms and show her the frying pan. She squirms until I finally set her down and let her run off for the television. She is not a morning person. No one is, except me, and that's because caffeine is my closest friend.

I am in my element, frying and toasting and scrambling and buttering. This is my dream life, set free in the kitchen, family rising around me, dog at my feet. I cook, therefore I am. We may not live in a college town, and my commute may sometimes resemble the trek across the Donner Pass (albeit without the cannibalism), but these are moments to be cherished. I am not so naïve (or arrogant) as to think my life is somehow more difficult than others, my road more complicated or twisted, my sadness more profound or noteworthy. On a relative scale, every day is a dream, every minute a blessing. I count them while I can.

Christine kisses me good morning, then pours herself some coffee. Simon plunks himself down in front of the sports pages. Lulu wanders in from the family room, the smell of breakfast drawing her away from the television. "Are the home fries ready?" she asks.

"Ready, freddy," I say.

I scoop out the potatoes, serve the eggs, pour more coffee. My family digs in eagerly. The sound of scraping forks and clinking glasses is as delicious as a four-star meal.

"Dad," says Lulu finally. "You should cook in a diner."

It is, I realize, the highest compliment. Paid to a father by his loving, and hungry, daughter.

"More home fries, please," she adds.

I fill her plate high with potatoes and squirt a moat of ketchup around them. She salts them like a famished trucker while I admire my handiwork, the happy genius of my household. The sun streams through the kitchen windows. Dust motes float lazily in the air. Lulu raises a potato, sticks it in her mouth, and eats.

Dinner with Grandma

My mother could not cook. The only child of immigrants, she was too immersed in school, career, and feminism to be bothered by the niceties of the kitchen. Besides, my grandmother was an excellent cook, specializing in Old World delicacies like stuffed cabbage, chopped liver, and gefilte fish, who rarely traveled without a secret stash of cashew nuts or kohlrabi slices and, later, a pocketful of mint candies for her grandchildren. Though they had little money, my grandparents' table was never empty, and my mother managed to grow up in blissful ignorance of their financial status and the fundamentals of food preparation. Until she met my father.

He was a skinny, undernourished boy from Albany. Six foot four, he weighed only 155 pounds in high school. In part, this was a function of his metabolism, but it also reflected a sickly boyhood and an aversion to his own mother's cooking. When meat was served, my father refused to eat the fat, giving it to his stronger, faster, older brother who, according to family legend, at one point held the Illinois high school hundred-yard-dash record. My father was a picky eater before it was trendy to avoid cholesterol, trans fats, and glucose, which may explain, in part, his current good health.

When they married, just after my mother's twentieth birthday and her college graduation, she realized, with a sinking feeling familiar to those who dream they have forgotten to study for an exam, that she was responsible for meal preparation. Although my father had limited expectations, and a limited palate, my mother set to work learning how to poach an egg with the kind of grim determination she would later use to master enough French to pass her boards. Bolstered by her initial success, she proceeded to cook poached eggs for three straight days until she had emptied the carton.

I don't recall many memorable meals from my own childhood. There was a paella my mother learned from some hippie cookbook.* She also made a pot roast that lasted for two or three nights, the meat disintegrating further with each subsequent serving. "Pasta" had not yet been invented, but we had spaghetti with sauce from a jar, supplemented with sautéed onions, peppers, mushrooms, and hamburger. Weekends, my grandmother often cooked, frying chicken, chopping liver, serving warm "drinking" Jell-O that sent my brother, sister, and me into sugar-induced hysteria. Mostly, though, what I remember about dinner is that we ate it together. My father, an academic scientist, always returned from Brooklyn by six P.M., a commute he made from our house on Long Island for more than forty-five years. When someone missed dinner, it was usually my mother, who, later in life, returned to school to get her Ph.D. On those nights, she would leave a chicken with instructions to my father on how to bake it ("Place in oven at 350 degrees for 45 min-

---

* Antiwar activists, my parents took us to march on Washington at least half a dozen times in my childhood. Photographs of my mother from that time show her with long brown hair and John Lennon glasses, giving peace a chance, declaring that war was not healthy for children and other living things.

utes"), or he would buy us sausage pizza from the Roslyn Café, which to this day remains one of the highlights of my culinary life.

Of course, back then my father could afford to live twenty miles from work on a professor's salary. His job gave him summers off and required little travel, and he owned a house that cost a reasonable fraction of his modest paycheck. There were no Little League games that ran until 7:45 P.M., no "travel" teams or weekday practices. We didn't have tutors, or "enhanced" curricula, and our music lessons did not require bimonthly "recitals." Dance, gymnastics, acting, and art were activities restricted to the classroom, and no one traveled to Manhattan for special instruction or coaching. We rode our bicycles up the block, and at dinnertime we rode them home again.

We lived the American dream, the reason my grandparents immigrated to the United States in the first place: to give their children a better life and their grandchildren a chance for a house and a yard. But beneath the placid suburban exterior, a revolution was already taking place.

In the early 1950s, C. A. Swanson & Sons found itself with an oversupply of turkeys. Gerry Thomas, a salesman, inspired by the aluminum trays used by Pan Am for its in-flight meals, came up with the idea of packaging the turkey into a three-compartment tray and selling it as a "TV dinner."* Indeed, the box was designed

---

Clarence Birdseye is often credited as the "father of frozen foods" for his discovery that quick-freezing improved the taste and quality of frozen food. (An adventurous eater, Birdseye once claimed, "I ate about everything . . . beaver tail, polar bear and lion tenderloin. And I'll tell you another thing—the front half of a skunk is excellent.") In 1945, Maxson Food Systems manufactured early frozen meals called "Strato-Plates," which were complete meals reheated for airline passengers. In 1952 both Quaker State Foods and Frigi-Dinners began selling frozen meals on the retail market. It was Swanson's marketing clout, however, and the phrase "TV Dinner," which some credit to Gilbert and Clarke Swanson, that in 1954 led to the explosion in growth of frozen meals.

to look like a TV screen. Early print advertisements show a busy mother returning home with a bag of TV dinners and the caption "I'm late—but dinner won't be!"

At about the same time, a hamburger chain in Southern California was just getting started, as chronicled by Eric Schlosser in his book *Fast Food Nation*. Soon, America was filled with McDonald's, Burger King, Wendy's, Denny's, Friendly's, KFC, Jack in the Box, Subway, Taco Bell, Applebee's, and Chili's. This coincided with a rise of women in the workforce and the rapid development of the suburbs. Meanwhile, families were enjoying ice cream scooped into its own edible container, fruit drinks frozen on a stick, corn flakes, chop suey, Kool-Aid, Jell-O, Velveeta, peanut butter, tuna fish, pineapple slices, chocolate chip cookies, canned meat, canned soup, canned vegetables, casseroles, Crisco, and Tang. In short, our grandparents were raising a generation of children who did not know how to cook, couldn't be bothered to do it, and were affirmatively encouraged to avoid it. Cooking was not only time-consuming and messy, it was practically antifeminist, subjecting women to the physical confines of the kitchen and the intellectual strictures of food preparation. Is it any wonder my own mother couldn't boil an egg?

To her credit, however, my mother was a health nut before it became a trend. There were no sugary treats in our house, no salty snacks, no Fritos, Doritos, or Lay's. While other kids got Oreos in their lunch bags, we got apple slices and carrots, which caused me endless embarrassment and were impossible to trade during lunchtime. Soda was poison, as far as my mother was concerned, as were alcohol and sugar.* My brother had a friend whose parents

---

* My mother, however, smoked cigarettes during this entire time and was a manic consumer of caffeine.

owned a separate freezer just for ice cream and kept a drawer brimming with fruit roll-ups. This we considered heaven, while to my mother it deserved a special circle in Dante's hell. Later, his friend would pay with a constant weight problem.

I cared little for cooking, and I don't remember being particularly picky about my food choices (except for organ meats, which I abhorred). In college, I ate practically everything, with the kind of iron stomach required for a diet of hamburgers, hot dogs, Monte Cristo sandwiches, Cap'n Crunch cereal, and large tubs of peanut butter and ice cream. But perhaps because of my mother's nutritional values, and my father's attempts to do his share in the kitchen, after college I developed an interest in what I was eating. It began during the year I lived in Cape Cod, wrote fiction, shared a house with two friends, and learned how to dice an onion from the chef in the restaurant where I worked. By law school, I had become something of a "foodie," grinding my own coffee, buying fresh pasta, and searching for ingredients at the farmer's market. Although I still subsisted mostly on pizza, during my second and third summers of law school I worked for a Wall Street law firm and lunched at some of New York's finest restaurants. I developed a taste for calamari, escargot, and sushi, and could soon tell the difference between a dessert fork and a salad fork.

When I ventured back to my parents' house, I often did the cooking, particularly during the summer, when my brother and I would grill swordfish or tuna and I would make a side dish of risotto or linguine with white clam sauce. My sister was happy to eat a simple meal, but she did not cook, and my mother avoided the kitchen if she could. Like many upper-middle-class adults of their generation, my parents' food tastes had changed as nutritional information became available. The pot roasts and hamburgers of my youth were supplanted by salmon, sea bass, and salads. Now my mother could often be found snacking on rice cakes and

raw vegetables, and it was difficult to locate anything in their refrigerator that contained cholesterol, including butter, milk,
cheese, or eggs. Lactaid was my father's drink of choice, sparkling
water my mother's. Their cupboards were often bare or contained
ingredients long out of date, while the food in their freezer required nuclear fission to thaw. Indeed, after raising three children,
they seemed content to stop cooking, relying on foraging, takeout,
and the kindness of strangers.

There was, however, one exception to their nouvelle minimal-
ist meal philosophy. Several times a year, on Thanksgiving, Passover, and the Jewish High Holidays, my parents' shelves would be
stocked with ingredients, my mother would buy the half and half
she knew I took in my coffee, and sticks of real butter appeared in
the refrigerator. Although she deigned to delegate a side dish to
Christine and a salad to my cousin, for the most part my mother
kept control of the holiday menu, reserving to herself the turkey
and stuffing, matzo ball soup, sweet potatoes, kasha *varnishkes,*
and chocolate mousse pie.*

Which was fine by me.

Loaded down with enough mashed potatoes to sink the *Ti-
tanic,* we corral our children and dog into the car for the trip across
the Sound to my parents' house.

"Next year, we're doing this at our house," says Christine.

"You don't mean that," I say.

"Why not?"

"First of all, our house isn't big enough." My parents' dining
room is nearly three times larger than ours, and their kitchen is

---

* At Passover and Yom Kippur she usually substituted Cornish game hens for the
turkey, *kugel* for the sweet potatoes, and added gefilte fish to the menu. There
was also always a non-meat option for Christine—salmon or sea bass—which
my father prepared with his signature mustard and caper sauce.

modern and bright while we can only dream of renovating. "Plus, the last thing I want to do is clean a hundred pots."

"Your mother hires someone. We could, too."

"It's expensive."

"It's not that expensive."

"Anyway, she'll never let it go."

Christine nods, silently acknowledging what we both know to be true. This, more than anything, is the reason we continue to have dinner at Grandma's on the major holidays. To give it up, my mother would have to acknowledge she is no longer the provider, the caretaker, the watcher over her brood. She has come a long way since the days she poached her first egg, becoming more like her own mother every year.

"Thanksgiving is my favorite holiday," says Lulu. Mine, too. Political correctness aside, it is the one holiday most of us can share, requiring no heavy religious observation, just a serious commitment to eating.

When we arrive, the kitchen windows are already steamed with pots boiling, birds cooking, sauces reducing. Lulu runs into Grandma's arms, while Grandpa gives Simon a big hug.

"Have you grown?" Grandpa asks. It is a rhetorical question. Simon grows like a weed in a vacant lot—without restraint, and only a shaggy mop on top to measure the distance. He shrugs, then runs off for the basement with Lulu in hot pursuit, both eager to use my parents' treadmill, which they consider a giant toy for their amusement.

My brother, sister, and cousins have yet to arrive, so we share family gossip while my father bastes the turkey and my mother stirs the soup. Christine finishes setting the table, and I gather the liquor to set up the bar. Being in my parents' house, the house in which I grew up, makes me feel both claustrophobic and cared for, as if I am thirteen again, struggling to escape my parents' rules yet secretly craving them. I wander about downstairs, looking at old photographs, noting how the paint has peeled in the living room and the master bath needs new tile. The house is like an old friend I see so often that I barely register how much he's aged—but he has grown older, I can see it now, his lines deepened and his color faded. The renovations I thought so recent are actually a decade old, in need of renovation themselves.

Upstairs, the bedrooms have been redecorated since we went to college, but the rooms still hold our younger selves. My desk drawers brim with photographs, trinkets, yearbooks, and other mementos of elementary and high school life. There are report cards, book reports, even an old copy of my SAT scores. Extra copies of my book about law firm life, *Double Billing,* fill the shelves, next to high school classics like *The Catcher in the Rye, To Kill a Mockingbird,* and *A Separate Peace.* In the closet there are newspapers announcing President Nixon's resignation, dog-eared copies of *Mad* magazine, and, incongruously, Christine's wedding dress, boxed up and shoved in a corner where we left it when we went on our honeymoon.

I find a photograph of myself playing guitar in a band, wearing a Boston T-shirt with hair nearly to my shoulders. I slip the photo from the bedroom like an ancient artifact and take it downstairs to show my children. They marvel at my hair (and the fact that I still had some), and Lulu wants to know whether she has Boston on her iTunes (she does). Simon tells me he has run a mile on the treadmill. With his untucked shirt, bare feet, and rumpled hair, he looks like an extra from *The Endless Summer,* riding his surfboard in his grandparents' basement. He's about to get back on for another mile when the doorbell rings and we hear my sister's voice, then Sugar barking. The kids dash up the stairs because they know their three-year-old cousin Ari has arrived from Newton. I switch off the treadmill, then join them.

The foyer is crowded with new arrivals and dogs. Sugar plays with Mona, my sister's mutt, who barks at her with the kind of cranky annoyance the elderly muster for a silly puppy. The human adults exchange hugs and kisses, while the children quickly run off for the basement and the toys. "Don't let him on the treadmill!" I call to Simon, which might be a metaphor, but is meant literally. My sister wonders whether she should follow them downstairs, but I tell her she can trust Simon. It seems like yesterday we were childproofing our own apartment against this energetic boy who was so anxious to walk he crawled like Quasimodo, one leg extended as if trying to raise himself to his feet. Now, here he is, another boy in his charge, wishing for a younger brother so he can teach him baseball.

My own brother arrives next, and then my cousins, adding three more children to the mix, but no dogs. Soon we are eighteen, as friends of my parents arrive. "The more the merrier" is my mother's philosophy. Though we accuse her of overdoing it every year, the truth is we are pleased to be part of a crowd. We are not a fecund family: My mother is a single child; my father has one brother; my brother is childless. We have barely managed to reproduce ourselves. In Italy, we would be eligible for financial assistance. In China, we would be Communist party members. Yet when we gather around the big table in the dining room, we are like something from a Woody Allen movie: verbal, vociferous, and intent on eating as much as possible.

The usual doctor and lawyer jokes are exchanged. The J.D.s outnumber the M.D.s, but the doctors have the unaligned parties on their side: the educators, scientists, and spouses. It's not that either side really has anything against the other; it's just that a good-natured joshing is our way of counting our blessings, thanking the gods for the bounty before us. Children and dogs run beneath our feet, and at some point one of them gets stuck, which requires disengagement, extrication, the Jaws of Life. My mother insists that my father give a toast, and he raises his glass and says something heartfelt yet unmemorable, a warm expression of love and joy that a man in his eighth decade, born into a generation where fathers were seen but rarely heard, might say. My sister and I exchange glances, telepathically communicating our love for our father, our appreciation of his steady presence in our lives, his unswerving dedication to home, hearth, and family. This is a man who could eat poached eggs for nearly a week straight without complaint. Let that be a lesson for me.

When the meal is finally eaten and the last plates have been brought into the kitchen, where my parents' housekeeper and her daughter rinse them clean and place them in the dishwasher, there are several observations worth making. First, stuffing is definitely better when it has a healthy dose of chestnuts and has been cooked inside the turkey (rather than in a pan, as Christine must suffer for her vegetarian sins). This year's stuffing is among the best, owing in large part to the aforementioned chestnuts. Also, you can never have too many carbohydrates. In addition to the stuffing, Christine's mashed potatoes, matzo balls, and sweet potatoes, we have bread, noodles, and a cranberry-orange compote. Finally, dessert is essential. Just when you think you can't eat any more, it's crucial to have three kinds of pie, chocolate mousse, cheesecake, cookies, and my favorite, tiramisu.

After we've eaten ourselves into a food coma, those of us who can still ambulate retreat to the family room for the obligatory viewing of Laurel and Hardy's *March of the Wooden Soldiers,* a Thanksgiving favorite. While Stan and Ollie flee from the bogeymen, there are several disagreements among family members over matters trivial and small. But all ends well when the bogeymen are driven back into the gator-filled bog and peace and domestic tranquillity are restored.

A footrace for the best rooms ensues, followed by a lengthy game of musical beds, and then a steely battle of wills as our children try to outlast us, popping up like prairie dogs while we knock them back down. Finally, exhausting both them and ourselves, we fall into a long and tryptophan-induced sleep, dreaming of giant birds offering corn to Pilgrims.

In the morning, it's leftovers for breakfast (the cheesecake tastes even better after it has been left out all night), and then several hours of shopping and moviegoing before returning to my parents' for more leftovers. My brother departs for his Upper East Side apartment, but my sister, her husband, and their son spend another night, and we decide to join them. At this point, not much turkey remains, but there are plenty of carbohydrates, including dessert, and after stuffing ourselves again, we vow never to touch another piece of pie.

Thanksgiving truly is the great, secular American holiday, where we get to give thanks for eating more food in a day than many people get to eat in a month. But as I load the car on Sunday morning, making room in the trunk for baggies of matzo balls and noodles, I put aside my cynicism for twenty-four hours and thank God (or Darwin, or whomever) for my family. Crazy, annoying, exasperating, and just plain nutty, they are mine, and I love them, and I wouldn't have them any other way.

Will Work for Food

On the road again.

Or should I say stuck on the road again. I wait in the airport at Kansas City for the 6:35 P.M. flight to New York. It is now 7:45 P.M. and the plane shows no inclination to take off any time soon. I have missed two meals at home this week, and if this plane doesn't leave tonight, it's possible I may miss a third. I tap away at my BlackBerry, check my voice mail, and send a text message. Finally, when it seems that I have exhausted the limits of technology, and just when I'm getting ready to make another hotel reservation, the pilot asks the flight attendants to take their seats and announces we are cleared for departure.

I settle back in my seat and look out the window. The ground rushes past, and the crush of gravity weighs me down as the plane ascends into the sky. I have avoided thinking about the inevitable for nearly four months, but it's not disappeared, just gone underground for a temporary reprieve. Although I have tried my best to work two jobs, to be all things to all people, there are physical limits to finite things, laws of time, space, and matter. A man cannot be in three places at the same time.

And just like that, I realize the inevitable: I have to quit.

It's not as if I haven't known this since the beginning. In some respects I have deliberately forced myself into this situation, choosing a course I knew would lead to loss of at least one job. By pledging myself to dinner, I forswore all those things that kept me away. For a few months I have chosen to ignore the inevitable, but I cannot ignore it any longer. I am neither a good father nor a good employee when I am traveling between two worlds.

I make some quick financial calculations: If I continue teaching and writing, I should be able to squeak through to the summer without tapping into my home equity line of credit. After that, I am likely to run out of money, but in a pinch I believe I could get some work from my old law firm or former clients. We won't starve. The point is I have committed to making dinner with my family. Until school ends, that is my charge. I must find a way to make it work, even if it means going into debt. Maybe I will discover that it is impossible for a man to pay the bills and have a family life, but until I've given it the year I said I would, I cannot accept failure.

By the time we land in New York, I am clear about my decision. One family. One home. One job.

Christine is awake when I arrive home, the lights still shining from the upstairs bedroom. I leave my bags in the kitchen and climb the stairs.

"I couldn't sleep," she says.

"It's late," I say. She hands me her glasses, and I lay them on the nightstand.

"How was your trip?"

"I'm quitting."

"Really?" She does not sound surprised.

"I have to."

She nods. "How will we manage?"

"We'll manage."

Christine has always trusted me, although my decisions have not always been the most well-reasoned. Yet somehow we have come this far: two beautiful children, a safe home, good health insurance.

"I wish there were a way you could do both jobs."

I don't know exactly how to explain to Christine that I cannot continue with half-measures. I do nothing well when I try to do everything adequately. In trying to satisfy everyone, I end up pleasing no one. I feel the way I did when I decided to leave my first law firm job and go to Iowa City to pursue an M.F.A. in fiction writing so many years ago. Against the advice of my parents, and even some of my friends, I took an absurd leap that ended up as the best decision I ever made. Since then, life has filled with gradual accretions, bits of meaningless fluff, until I came to barely recognize the person I once was. The point of Dinner with Dad was to get back to that place, to focus on the truly important things and to discard the peripheral. Like writing a formal poem, I have set rules in order to surprise myself with where they might lead.

"I took that class from Jorie, too," says Christine, referring to our favorite professor at Iowa. "But how will we pay the bills?"

I explain the finances to her, although she still seems dubious. "I was going to quit three months ago," I continue.

"But you've been working from home, and it's been working out."

"No. It hasn't." My eighty-hour weeks have morphed into sixty-hour weeks and sometimes, heaven forbid, forty-hour weeks. Sooner or later, it will catch up to me. Better to quit before I am fired.

"And then what?"

"Dinner."

I'll say this for my wife: She's not a nagger. She worries, but mostly she keeps her concerns to herself. Although some have mistaken this for serenity, I know she obsesses over little things, tiny details substituting for larger issues. When she's feeling particularly stressed, she falls asleep. Now, she announces she's exhausted, and switches off her light.

"Christine," I say. "This is really the best thing for all of us."

"I know."

"It'll work out; you'll see."

"Good night."

She rolls over, and in about thirteen seconds she is asleep. I am exactly the opposite, and even though I've been going since six A.M., I toss and turn for about an hour before falling into a fitful sleep.

In the morning, I wake early, make coffee, then stay late and walk the kids to the bus stop. After two nights in Kansas City, seeing them again reminds me why I'm doing what I'm doing.

"Will you be home early or late?" Simon asks.

"Early," I promise.

He gives me a kiss before he runs onto the bus.

" 'Bye, daddy!" calls Lulu as she follows him.

Watching the two of them race for their seats—Simon at the back, Lulu at the front—nearly breaks my heart. Five years ago, when Simon boarded this bus for the first time, his face at the window reflected my own emotions: forlorn, lonely, and confused. Now, they are both so old, confident, and sure. They don't even look back for me. Instead, I see Simon jumping up and down in the back seat with several of his friends, while Lulu and her best friend appear locked in an intense conversation. When I think of leaving Westport, these are the images I struggle over. The costs of moving, I understand, are high. If I offered my children a choice—dinner with Dad or their friends—I'm not sure I would be happy with their answer. Father knows best, but only thirty years later, from a great distance, after much reflection and psychotherapy.

Christine has shut herself in her office when I get home. I can take a hint. I gather my belongings and head for Starbucks. I find a table near the window, plug in my iPod, and boot up my laptop. It's laughable, really, the number of things I am trying to juggle, but I have begun to get a little clarity. With my word processing program open, I make a list titled "Important," and write: 1) family, 2) writing, 3) exercise, 4) free time, 5) money. I do not place health on the list, or God, or country, because I consider them mostly beyond my control. I contemplate swapping exercise with free time, but decide that given a choice I would rather go for a run.

I am not surprised, really, to have placed money fifth on the list. Although I believe I enjoy the good life as much as the next guy, when I think hard about trading it for family, writing, exercise, or free time, I can't. If I could, I wouldn't have gone to Iowa in the first place, but would have stayed at the law firm to make my fortune. What is money but a stand-in for all the other things in life that are important? By itself, it's worthless; it has value only in what it can purchase for us: gadgets, travel, cars, houses. If it were possible to have things of value without money, we wouldn't need it.* Sitting there with my list in front of me, I realize most of

---

* To some extent, of course, money can "buy" free time because we can use money to hire a housecleaner or a painter or other person to do our chores. Strictly speaking, however, money does not buy time; it buys other things that can free up time. Making money to buy free time also costs time—sometimes more time than we can actually purchase, given that time is limited by physical laws but money is not.

the things I enjoy best don't require money. I am not the kind of person who takes pleasure in driving around in a fancy sports car, or who needs to go on expensive vacations, or who wants to make his home a showcase of luxurious trinkets. Don't get me wrong: I don't wear sackcloth. I would jump at the opportunity to go to Venice or St. Barths (if someone else were paying). And I still have to pay the mortgage and the gas, electric, phone, and cable bills. But once the necessities are covered, I'm pretty happy if I can toss a ball in the front yard with Simon or go for a swim with Lulu.

Fifteen years ago I never would have needed reminding. I lived as a student longer than most of my friends. I valued reading, writing, running, free time more than most, and did whatever I could to pursue them. It seemed to me then that life was too short to race into full-time employment, marriage, a middle-class existence. My first job seemed like a lark, a mistake, something I fell into by accident and from which I couldn't wait to extricate myself, which I did within a year. When I returned to New York from Iowa City, my friends wanted to know when I would grow up,* which only confirmed the rightness of my choices. I was twentyeight; I had no plans to grow up any time soon.

But time flies when you're having fun. Or not.

After two happy hours spent writing, I leave Starbucks. Although I'd like to avoid it, I know I have to call my boss. Because I am banned from the house, and do not have a local office, I call him from my cell phone in the car. He is not shocked, just disappointed, to hear my decision. He makes one last effort to convince me that moving to Kansas City is the answer to my problems. It

* The fact that my girlfriend was five years younger than I seemed to confirm my essential immaturity.

might be, if Christine or I had family in the Midwest. As it is, I can't see uprooting my wife and children for a better commute.

I feel lighthearted and at ease. Am I crazy? I have just given up a good job with a good company, a move that has possible long-term career implications and serious financial consequences. I remind myself, however, that I already have one job that I like, and also a commitment to dinner that requires presence, not absence. What kind of father do I want to be? What kind of memories do I want to create for my children? When I packed my U-Haul truck many years ago, I had no guaranteed source of income, no assurances for the future. I barely had a house. Trusting my instincts, however, I drove west.

Now I head south on the Post Road, equally uncertain of the future, but heading in that direction. I am blessed with a loving family, supportive parents, a J.D. degree. I will never be homeless, or hungry, or unable to afford medical care. I will never fear wild animals or fight off savages. The difference between risk and adventure, I understand, is a matter of freedom to choose between the two. My grandparents traveled in the hold of a cargo ship to a country where they could not speak the language. They worked eighteen-hour days to put their children through school. They died young, back-broken and bone-tired. I am simply coming home for dinner.

I stop to buy a sandwich at Gold's, one of the few businesses in town that remind me of an earlier era, when stores had one-syllable names, pronounceable and approachable, and didn't smell of lavender and tea tree oil. The sandwich comes with a half-sour pickle (of course) and chips that are neither old-fashioned nor newfangled, but simply crisp and salty. I take my sandwich to the library and eat it in the reading room while preparing my notes for teaching. With the Saugatuck River as my background, I almost feel like I live in a different era, languid and dreamy, perched on a riverbank in Peaceful, New England.

After several hours, however, I return to the modern world, to the Internet, e-mail, and voice mail. Unfortunately, the electronic pipeline does not stop for one man's fantasy. It spits out digits indifferently, oblivious to peace, sanity, daydreams. No matter how quickly I respond to any single message, another pops up, like flies to be swatted. Because the day is too nice to be ruined with work, and because I feel as if I have something to celebrate, I shut off my computer and go shopping.

My destination is Stop & Shop, where I know I can waste plenty of time in the cavernous aisles. The vast choices give me the illusion that I can make anything, cook any meal, even if most of the products are canned, carbonated, or combustible. I am the only man in the supermarket, except for a couple of retirees, which I don't realize until several women have given me the once-over. I see myself in their eyes: ragged jeans, T-shirt, baseball cap. Although the economy has picked up, Westport and nearby Weston and Wilton still have their share of dot-com refugees, men who left their investment banks to strike it rich on the Internet. When the bubble burst, so did their dreams, and sometimes their homes. We know of several couples who divorced and moved, unable to weather the economic stress. The wary looks I receive as I walk the aisles makes me realize these shoppers think I'm unemployed. At first, I want to laugh, enjoying my disguise, my secret life. Then I remember the men I knew, who probably thought they could do no wrong until the financial pressure got to them, the months of going without a paycheck, and their formerly idyllic lives fell apart.

Suddenly I feel like shouting: I'm a good father! I'm working, *and* cooking! I'm making good choices! But my smiles are not returned, and the women scurry away, leaving me to shuffle alone down the frozen food aisle.

Why should they embrace me? Perhaps I am jeopardizing my family. Perhaps I should be out in the world, worshipping the mighty greenback, bringing home the bacon, stuffing the family socks. What kind of man gives up a sure thing to cook dinner? What kind of father risks economic collapse to butter some bread? While most of the men I know express a desire to spend more time with their families, few are doing much to make it a reality, and most are sneaking off to play golf when they can.* Many of the mothers would, too, if they could. One friend of mine, when I told her what I was doing, expressed incredulity that it could even be considered a "project." "It's what I do every day," she said.

Then I turn the corner and run into Jana, the mother of a friend of my son's. With her corkscrew red hair, she is the closest Westport has to a "character," the kind of woman who would be an actress or run her own jewelry company in New York, but here she manages three kids and does yoga.

"I read your blog," she says, referring to the online diary I've been keeping of my dinners. "I think it's fabulous!"

"Pshaw," I say, which is meant to sound ironic but comes off sounding genuinely hokey.

"Don't get discouraged," she continues. "They'll come around, you'll see."

"Did I sound discouraged? I didn't mean to."

"Can I give you a suggestion?" she asks. I nod. "Keep it simple. Kids aren't impressed with all those fancy meals. They just want simple."

---

* When given a choice to trade money for more time, according to Arlie Russell Hochschild in *The Time Bind,* most prefer not to. In law firms that offer "flex time" and part-time arrangements to their lawyers, for example, almost none take it. Although there may be multiple explanations for this phenomenon, it appears that some of us would rather work than be with our families.

"I made macaroni and cheese," I say.

"Yes, but you used fancy cheese, and fancy pasta. I read that."

"Penne isn't fancy."

"It is if you're used to bunnies."

Jana has a short attention span, and after a moment she's telling me about her Christmas plans, which involve a lengthy trip to visit in-laws in Colorado she would rather avoid even though it promises lots of skiing and free babysitting. I try to muster some sympathy, but I cannot. Our Christmas plans are unformed, and definitely won't include any trips to any place we can't reach by car.

"Say hello to Christine," she says as she heads the other way with her shopping cart. "And keep up the cooking!"

Newly inspired, albeit somewhat chastened, I return to the frozen food section, where I spy a bag of edamame. Although edamame seem fancy, both kids have actually enjoyed them at our local Asian "bistro." Keeping with the Asian theme, I grab two packages of extra firm tofu, which is something I know they like. Tofu with edamame is a variation on one of the fifteen-minute recipes I haven't yet tried. Perhaps after two strikes, my third attempt will be a hit.

I buy the food, and several other ingredients I need, then return to my car and drive home. Fortunately, Christine is gone by now, so after I put the packages away, I work in my home office for the rest of the afternoon. At about five o'clock, I lose steam and wish they would come home so I could make dinner. That's the problem with a fifteen-minute meal—it really only takes fifteen minutes, and can't be prepared until everyone is present. At six, I call Christine on her cell phone, but she does not answer. Finally, at six-thirty, they arrive, cranky and hungry.

"What's for dinner?" Lulu asks.

"You'll see," I say, not wanting her to prejudge the meal.

I ask Christine if she'll set the table, and she wants to know why I haven't. This strikes me as reverse discrimination, the kind of thing that men are always accused of saying to their wives, just before getting clobbered by a frying pan.

"But you're making dinner," Christine protests.

"Exactly," I say.

Grudgingly, she subcontracts the job to Lulu, who is equally unhappy with the task. Simon has mysteriously vanished.

Turning to the stove, I melt a tablespoon of butter with several tablespoons of olive oil in a sauté pan. To this I add two cloves garlic and the tofu, cut into half-inch slices. I cook the tofu until it is browned on both sides, then add a cup of frozen edamame, and cook for about another three minutes. Just before serving, I squeeze in some soy sauce and a little cooking wine, then serve over prepackaged microwaveable rice. Presto! One home-cooked meal for busy dad and hungry family.

If only it were that easy.

Because here's the question I ask myself later—much later—after I've had an opportunity to thrash around downstairs, throwing a few pillows into the couch and tossing most of the food into the garbage: Am I really changing my life, or simply shaking it up, moving things about, solving some problems but creating new ones where none existed? Although there are other rooms in which people have had their way with me, no one has ever taken advantage of me in the kitchen before. I'd been overworked, yes, but at least when I came home everyone was asleep and no one pushed my vegetables desultorily around the plate until I got tired of trying to cajole them into tasting one damned soybean, or convincing them that tofu is meant to be cooked. Is Dinner with Dad a net gain, I wonder, or just a reallocation of resources? Or, to put it another way, by coming home for dinner, have I just created one more space for conflict, anger, disappointment, and unhappiness?

Yes, I know, life is complicated. You can't really appreciate your parents until you become a parent yourself. Sometimes the seeds you plant won't take root for decades. Two steps forward, one step back. Blah, blah, blah.

As for dinner, your kids won't eat it, but at least your wife will, even if she doesn't want to talk with you anymore.

Whining and Dining

The fact of the matter is I don't understand food issues, although I know that many people have them. In high school I knew plenty of girls who spent their lunchtime with their fingers down their throats. Ditto college. These days my sister seems to survive on Cheetos, my wife won't eat anything that had eyes (except the occasional small piece of salmon), and most of my former girlfriends seemed to do a lot of picking and pushing of the food on their plates. Interestingly, I don't think I know a single man with food issues, although I'm sure they exist.

If someone wants to explain why my wife and children, who like shrimp (except for Lulu), black beans, peppers, and tortillas, can't eat a dish that is essentially all of those ingredients, I would appreciate it. Personally, I think they are being silly, and when they refuse to eat my food, I don't handle it well. Take my shrimp and black bean fajitas, for example (please!). For these, I marinated shrimp, red and yellow peppers, and onions in olive oil, soy sauce, lime juice, garlic, oregano, basil, cayenne, pepper, and salt. I cooked everything on high heat in a cast-iron skillet, and added a can of rinsed black beans just when it was almost ready. Then I warmed one plate of tortillas, and voilà, delicious!

Except no one thought so. For Lulu, Christine picked out a few black beans and rolled her a burrito, which Lulu didn't touch. Simon made a valiant effort to pretend he liked it, but he left most of what I served him on his plate (this from a boy who will eat two of my black bean burritos). Even Christine ate a small amount, then went to the kitchen to retrieve a chocolate chip scone she claimed she had been craving.

What went wrong? According to Christine, "mixing" the peppers with the shrimp made the dish unappetizing. Call me crazy, but I think if a person eats shrimp or black beans and the same person eats peppers, mixing them together shouldn't make the result inedible.

But maybe that's just me.

My students are taking finals, and they think the stress level is unbearable. We all know, however, how much more stressful life becomes as you get older. In school, you have only yourself to consider, only your own mouth to feed. You think you have financial problems, but you don't even know what it means to pay the bills until you receive two dozen a month, you can't eat pizza for breakfast, lunch, and dinner to skimp pennies, and there's no such thing as deferring payment on your loans (unless you declare bankruptcy). Stress?

In the postgraduate world you can't sleep until noon and stay out until two A.M. You can't decide to blow off a class and get the notes from someone else. You can't plunk yourself down with a textbook for ten hours straight, ignoring everything else in your life including loved ones. You can't watch TV when you want to, enforce silence when you need to, leave on a trip when you feel like it, sleep with someone just for the heck of it, avoid them when they annoy you, go home to do your laundry, rifle someone else's refrigerator, complain that there's nothing to eat (and have someone go get it for you), leave your clothes on the floor, your dishes in the sink, and your books and papers spread across the table like a tornado swept through them. You can't claim the dog ate your homework, a worm ate your hard drive, a virus made you do it. You can't drink foolishly, relentlessly, heedless of the consequences. You can't take off for three weeks after finishing your exams, confident there's nothing and nobody waiting for you, shutting off your BlackBerry (you don't even own a BlackBerry), refusing to answer your e-mail, and generally disappearing from the clamoring world.

You can't do any of these things because you are a parent, a father, a husband, and a provider, and you have taken a vow. Thus, as perturbed as I am by my family's reluctance to mix and match, I know I must go on. This is, after all, the whole point of publicly declaring your intentions, like standing up at Yankee Stadium and making a marriage proposal. The more witnesses, the more egg on your face.

It is also, in part, the point of keeping a blog about my progress. I feel goaded by regular readers into completing the year. Every time I post something about my frustration or disillusionment, I get responses like this:

PLEASE . . . enough with the bad dad thing, OK? Let's see how you do on the dad test:

A. Are you taking responsibility for your kids? Supporting them? Providing money so they don't need welfare or AFDC or WIC?

B. Are you there? Are you helping to raise the kids? Parenting them? Are you married to their mom, making a family? Are you employed, working, providing a good role model?

C. Are you abusing your kids? Any coat hangers, studded belts, Bunsen burners, or chains involved in their punishments?

D. Are you sending the kids to bed hungry because you can't afford to feed them (as thousands of single parents will be doing tonight)?

Okay, so he has a point: I should stop the whining and dining.

Like my students, however, I believe the immediate tasks before me are more difficult than anything anyone else has ever had to accomplish. Cooking dinner for my children? Impossible! Outrageous! Shocking! Never mind that my wife has been doing it for nearly a decade, and that legions of parents do it every day. My own struggles with my children's taste buds are unique, inimitable, and culturally significant. If I can't get them to appreciate my shrimp and black bean fajitas, then Western civilization is sure to collapse. It's the end of the world as we know it. Someone call Francis Fukuyama.

Fortunately, however, I do not have to cook every day, and for the next few days my wife provides much-needed relief. All I have to do is get myself home by six o'clock, and the table is set, food is cooking, and the kids are ready to eat. Although it's closer to *I Love Lucy* than *Leave It to Beaver*, this program is a wonderful thing, even if Christine can't always locate the salt or finds it easier to serve potatoes fifteen minutes before anything else is ready. Her cooking techniques tend toward the haphazard and slapdash. She prefers to use a serrated bread knife to cut vegetables, for which she will be lashed with a wet noodle by Wolfgang Puck, and when she sautés in a nonstick pan she uses—gasp!—a metal spatula.

She has her tricks, however. Maybe it's a gender thing, or a biochemistry thing, or just gradual acculturation, but Christine does not get easily frustrated when the kids don't eat her food. She is more willing to compromise, to have them try a bite, then microwave pasta if they won't eat it. She is also more likely to cook food the kids will eat and not make a big production out of preparing it. She makes pizza with store-bought frozen dough, and lets the kids roll their own. In this way, Lulu creates a giant rectangular pizza with a thick crust and lots of sauce and cheese that is actually quite yummy in its own fashion. More important, Simon has four slices and Lulu has two. Christine makes a separate red pepper and caramelized onion pizza for us, which I barely get to eat because I'm so filled with Lulu's pizza.

I can't help but feel jealous of her success, and a little resentful that she has "cheated" by buying dough. These are ridiculous thoughts, of course, but I'm not a proud man. I still see dinner as a competitive event, where the winner is the one who cooks best and longest and leaves the biggest mess. Cooking, for me, has always been a way to tame the beast, silence the doubters, and win the girl. As a former varsity track captain, I believe getting a head start is grounds for disqualification. Never mind that there is an entire industry devoted to cheating—from gourmet food shops that prepackage "meals to go" to supermarkets that sell premade pizza sauce and preshredded pizza cheese (a combination of mozzarella, Asiago, and Parmesan) to outfits like "Dream Dinners," "Super Suppers," and "Let's Eat!" that select, chop, and premeasure ingredients for busy parents to combine on-site and freeze into dishes like "beef kabobs with tomato Thai ginger sauce" and "apricot glazed pork chops with corn fritters," which can be heated at home, yielding the illusion of actual food preparation.* Some

---

* According to *The New York Times*, these "meal assembly centers" are big business, projected to earn about $270 million in 2006. They even have their own industry trade group, the Easy Meal Prep Association.

fast-food restaurants have taken convenience even further, bringing dinner directly to the car for easy conveyance home. Applebee's "Carside to Go," for example, provides a variation on the old drive-in restaurant by delivering meals that customers phone in and then pick up in dedicated parking spaces when they arrive.*

What's wrong with a little cheating, anyway, if it gets the family to sit down together? Buying spices, frozen vegetables, sliced bread—it's all cheating to some degree. We have grown so used to strawberries in the winter, bananas year-round, and butter, milk, and ice cream in convenient rectangular boxes, that to live any other way would seem hopelessly anachronistic.

But old habits die hard. Today's shortcuts are tomorrow's partially hydrogenated vegetable oils, convenience triumphing over common sense and good health. Remember I made my own ghee, reducing butter in a pan for more than an hour although I could have purchased it at any specialty food store or, heaven forbid, used canola oil. I am not entirely displeased, therefore, when our children refuse to eat popovers that Christine has prepared from a mix. I've never been a big fan of popovers, perhaps because I worked in a restaurant where they were served and ate too many during breaks. Large, eggy, misshapen. Which is exactly how they are viewed by Simon and Lulu. Christine's memories, however, are of steaming popovers with jam in her kitchen as a girl, and she is sorely disappointed that the children won't try them.

"Just one bite," she pleads with Lulu.

"No!" says Lulu.

"Then go to your room," says Christine.

---

* "Carside to Go" is the fastest growing part of Applebee's business, according to a company press release, and Valentine's Day the busiest day of the year for the service. Go figure.

So maybe she is not superhuman after all. Hell hath no fury like a parent whose food has been scorned.

"It's not funny," she says to me.

"Who's laughing?" I ask, covering my mouth.

Later, after Christine relents and lets the kids snack on Wheat Thins and string cheese, we bathe them and put them to bed early. I sit on Lulu's bed and kiss her goodnight.

"I don't like Mommy's food," she says.

"I don't love popovers, either," I admit.

"I like your food better."

Although I know this is just the ploy of a six-year-old playing her parents off each other, I can't help but feel flattered.

"What do you like best?" I ask, fishing for compliments.

"Fresh pasta," she says, without missing a beat.

"Maybe we'll have fresh pasta tomorrow," I say.

"Yes!" she says.

Then I kiss her again, and she grabs me around the neck until I have to pry her fingers apart. "Don't leave, Daddy!" she calls.

So I sit back down on her bed and hold one hand until I sense she is drifting to sleep. I remember how, as a baby, she used to fall asleep on my chest while we sat on the sofa in the living room. I would lift her gently and carry her back to the crib in the room she shared with her brother. Once asleep, nothing could wake her, a gene she inherited from her mother. Often, I would slip into our second bedroom and watch both children as they slept, their smooth brows and heavy-lidded eyes seemingly without a care in the world. It was at these moments I felt my role as father most keenly, these young lives who depended on me, not just for financial support, but for emotional and spiritual sustenance. Who they were, what they would be become, a function of who and what I was and how I lived.

Now, as I shut the door to Lulu's room, I have that same sense of wonder and trepidation. I may not be failing the Dad Test, but there is so much I don't know. What does it take to win the gold medal for fatherhood? Can I be both a good father and a good provider, earning enough money to give my children the material things I think they deserve? To get an A on the Dad Test, a father must do more than simply show up at the starting line. He must run the entire race, improve his pace, and finish with a good, swift kick.

"It's not a competition," says Christine as we sit in bed, a stack of exams in my hands.

"All dads are created equal," I say. "But some are more equal than others."

"George Orwell," she says. "*Animal Farm*."

I indicate the pile of papers on my lap. "These students all took the same class, listened to the same thing, read the same material. But some of them put more effort into their work, and they'll end up with better grades."

"Are you grading yourself?"

"Aren't the kids?"

"No. They love you. They're not grading you."

"Not with a pencil or pen. But they'll grow up, and remember. We all do."

Christine sighs. Before she married me, she did not own a set of measuring spoons. She used ordinary cutlery, and mixed ingredients by sight and feel. It was another one of our early fights.

"You already have an A. Just ask them."

"Did I have one last year?"

"You always had one. You're their father."

I know what she means, but find her answer unsatisfying. Clearly, there are good dads and bad dads and mediocre dads and superlative dads. A dad who loves his children but is never home cannot be a good dad, just as a dad who is always home but screams at his children is a bad dad. In between are the average dads, the ones whose children spend hours in therapy trying to tease out the threads, separating the traumatic from the merely annoying.

"What's the point, then, of getting home for dinner?" I ask.

"You tell me."

"I don't know. I thought I was doing it to be a better father."

"I thought you were doing it because you wanted to."

"I thought it was important to you, and to the kids."

"The only thing that's important to us is that you're happy."

"So you'd rather I didn't come home?"

Christine places her book on the bed, splayed open, spine up. She has been reading in voracious gulps, like a nomad at an oasis. Now she eyes me warily. "If coming home is going to make you angry, and you're going to take it out on the kids, then don't do it."

"*You* talking to *me*?"

"I had a bad night. I admit it. But I'm over it. You should get over it, too." She picks up her book and buries her face in the pages.

I wait for her to say something else, but when she doesn't, I return to my papers, circling the paragraphs with a heavy red pen. C, C, C−, B−. After my fourth subpar grade, I realize I am in no mood to be grading. I erase all my marks and resolve to start again in the morning. Then I find my own book, distracting myself with a story about a man who couldn't stay focused in the present moment and lived, instead, out of time, traveling between past and future until he vanished entirely. I fall asleep and dream of small boys chasing bicycles, wheels spinning brightly, always out of reach.

The next day, however, all is forgiven. Christine makes potato pancakes, and the kids love them. Greasy and hot, with applesauce and salt, the pancakes are the Jewish answer to fried dumplings, samosas, falafel, and a dozen other hot, greasy, lumpy things. Every culture and religion has one, or three, and the satisfying taste of starch fried in oil cures most ills, especially with a sprinkling of salt or sugar.

"These are like Grandma's," says Lulu, her face smeared with applesauce.

I know for a fact my mother uses the same mix as Christine, having purchased it myself several times. Right now, however, domestic loyalty seems more important than familial ties.

"Better than Grandma's," I say.

"Grandma's are burnt," says Simon.

I remember the joke Christine tells of the man who loved his mother's pot roast, until his wife finally gives in and gets his mother-in-law's recipe. When she prepares the roast perfectly, however, the man objects that it's not how his mother prepares it. Hers is burnt.

A mom can't win.

The advantage of being a dad, of course, is that expectations are low, any meal is a victory, and when the kids complain, you can storm out of the kitchen and threaten never to return.

"To Mom," I say. "She gets an A."

"A for 'awesome,' " says Lulu.

"A for 'amazing,' " says Simon.

"A for 'alluring,' " I say.

"What's 'alluring'?" asks Lulu.

"That's for me to know," I say, "and you to find out."

Pasties

Inspiration is a drug with a short half-life.

Four months into Dinner with Dad, and I already feel my commitment beginning to lag. What began with so much energy has begun to drag. It's the lack of motivation about meals, the absence of an appreciative audience, the sense that my children ought to be more thankful for my sacrifices, and my wife should, too. Instead, their lives seem to continue pretty much as they always have. If anything, I feel as if I'm getting in their way. While the kids used to have their after-dinner activities (PlayStation and television), now Dad intrudes and wants to know if Simon has really done his math homework. "Yes, Dad," he says, rolling his eyes, with the perfect insouciance only a tween can manage. This angers Christine as well because she has always supervised their homework (and the children have *never*—according to her—watched television or played PlayStation during the school week). They don't need me bossing them around, parachuting into their lives as if I'm going to repair everything that doesn't need fixing.

And another thing: It's not as if our dinner conversations have been so scintillating. All those studies about dinnertime being an opportunity for sharing and learning—who says so? Our meals have tended toward the brief and recalcitrant—that is, when I'm not losing my temper about something my kids won't eat. Simon will hop up from the table, or Lulu will, or neither will sit, or sit still, while any conversation tends toward the monosyllabic or the multispasmodic. It's enough to make a man want to eat his dinner in Grand Central with the bums, winos, and tourists.

Am I expecting too much from dinner? I just want my kids to rise from their seats, fall to their knees, and bless the grain and legumes I have bestowed upon them. I want my wife to sing my praises through the streets of Westport, to stop perfect strangers in the market and cry hosannas about the wonders of her husband. I am a man. I cook. Therefore, I rock.

I've made couscous and vegetables, sushi rice, biscuits and whole wheat bread. I've made split pea soup, fresh pasta, fried shrimp with batter and without. I've cooked pizza, burritos, and penne, added pesto and left it out. Yet despite the best ingredients, and best intentions, I'm as tired of my own cooking as I think my children are. No one is eating, and the only singing is my daughter's as she skips out of the kitchen after refusing to touch the carrots I've sautéed.

And about those studies. The most famous—the one cited repeatedly by well-meaning newspaper columnists and talk-show hosts—is the report by the National Center on Addiction and Substance Abuse (CASA) at Columbia University that seems to suggest eating dinner with your children will keep them away from drugs, drink, and substance abuse. In fact, what the CASA study demonstrates is not a causal link, but a correlation. It has almost as much significance as a study demonstrating that everyone who drank water between 1800 and 1820 is dead; therefore, drinking water must kill you. One of the largest failings of the CASA study is that it does not adjust for the age of the respondents. Not surprisingly, families that eat together more frequently tend to have younger children, while drug abuse is found more often in families with older children. Indeed, age correlates more strongly with the risk for drug abuse than does missing dinner. So does watching R-rated movies and having friends who are sexually active. The CASA study also fails to take into account a family's socioeconomic status, or whether the family itself has any history of drug use, factors that are much more closely linked to drug abuse than eating together.*

It is not with much regret, therefore, that I set aside my pots and pans for ten days for a trip to the Pacific Northwest to visit Christine's family. Although I won't be making dinner (at least I assume I won't), I decide that traveling with my family satisfies the rules for my project because I'm sure to be eating dinner with them every night. I'm looking forward, as well, to seeing in-laws and Christine's friends whom I haven't seen for a year or more.

The kids are excited, too, and insist on packing their own bags, which means Simon has more electronic equipment than a NASA engineer but no underwear, while Lulu has plenty of clothes but nothing that fits anyone larger than an American Girl. Christine and I "adjust" their suitcases after they've fallen asleep, replacing battery-operated devices with sweaters, and miniature

---

Many of these points were made by Carl Bialik, "The Numbers Guy," in his *Wall Street Journal* column (October 2005). He also notes that of a pool of 37,000 phone numbers, researchers reached only one thousand respondents, which, according to statisticians, is a very low response rate that does not adequately reflect teen substance abuse risk and probably explains why the study underrepresents black and Latino teenagers. Researchers also never asked respondents about their own drug use, but only about "risk factors" for drug use such as whether they knew anyone who used drugs.

stockings with the real thing. I am so intent on making sure they have the right clothes that I forget to pack socks for myself, and end up having to wear Simon's until I get to a department store two days after we arrive.

The first thing that strikes me when we land, as it always does, is how different the geography and topography of this landscape are: pine trees giving way to undulating fields of winter wheat and soybeans covering the Palouse. Also, how you can get an espresso at nearly every gas station. Before we reach our destination, Christine and I have already had two shots, and though we're buzzing, the kids are not. They're exhausted from a nine-hour journey that required waking at five A.M., changing planes in Minneapolis, and a two-hour drive from Spokane. We are all relieved when we pull into the driveway in Pullman, Washington.

I don't know how Ann does it.

Mother of four, keeper of five chickens, two cats, and one dog, and renovator of large Victorian on a hill overlooking Washington State University. Vegetarian, artist, mother, chef.

She steps from the house carrying her youngest, Mirabella, while our kids stand behind Christine sheepishly, awaiting introduction. Christine and Ann embrace, with the kind of fierce devotion of people who have known each other forever yet see each other infrequently. Ann is sturdy and compact, her hair cut bluntly, fingernails smooth, bereft of makeup. Her skin glows with a flawless beauty, olive on porcelain. She steps back and examines Christine, seems satisfied, then embraces her again.

Her children are wonders. The eldest, Ingmar, a certified genius, doing calculus at eleven. Now, at fifteen, he has exhausted the college curriculum and teaches himself Finnish from a textbook. He greets us with a formal bow, which sends Simon huddling even closer to his mother.

Within an hour, however, you would never know our children

were shy, or that Ann's children can speak three languages. They all play Mille Bornes on the living room floor while Christine, Ann, and I catch up in the kitchen. Ingmar laughs like a boy just entering adolescence as he and Simon trade cards.

At six o'clock, Ann's husband arrives. Born in Iran, he cuts a dramatic figure, and our kids seem slightly taken aback. It's easy to be frightened of Ali. Dressed all in Yohji Yamamoto, his curly hair cut in an *Eraserhead* buzz, two gold hoop earrings in each ear, black boots, black leggings, a black jacket, it's hard to imagine what his electrical engineering students must make of him. But as intimidating as he is on the outside, he is equally warm and fuzzy inside, prone to hugging and kissing. His long hands and fingers grasp wineglasses, books, and children's hands with the same reverent amazement at the things in this world.

"How are you?" he asks me, as if he hopes to sum up, in a single question, the meaning of life as we live it.

I give him the *Reader's Digest* version of the last two years, and he clucks about the travel and the hours. "Family is all that matters," he intones, with his heavy Mideastern accent. I don't disagree, but Ali is not one for subtlety of argument. He lives in a town where his house cost one-fourth the price of our home in Westport, while his academic salary is nearly the same as mine. His wife grew up in Pullman, and Ali has lived here since before he met her. Her parents, until recently, lived nearby, as does Ann's only brother. Although they have flirted with moving to Seattle, they seem newly content in their big house on the hill. Yes, family is all that matters, but what if your family lives in one of the most expensive real estate corridors in the world? What if your job requires you to travel nearly two hours in each direction? What if you want your children to have the best schools, the best teachers, the best access to theater, museums, music?

"My family is here," Christine says later, when we discuss it in bed after a delicious meal of *palak paneer* and *aloo matar gobi* with *dal* and *naan,* cooked by Ingmar and his sister, Ula, who are in an Indian food mood as of late. Christine is right, of course. We could sell our house in Westport and move to Idaho, buy another house without a mortgage, and live like kings. I might only see my parents, brother, and sister twice a year, but for the last thirteen years that's all we've seen of Christine's family. Why shouldn't we trade? Many years ago, when we first moved to Manhattan, Christine lobbied hard for Seattle. In the end, we agreed to try New York and see how it worked out. There we were, still trying.

The next night Ann makes eggplant and rice with curry while Ingmar stir-fries cabbage and makes egg rolls. Ula helps Ingmar wrap the egg rolls and consults on the proper spices, then crushes coriander with a mortar and pestle for Ann's curry. The meal is served on large white platters, steaming and fragrant, with plenty of opportunities to reach for another spoonful. Simon and Lulu pick at the rice, while Ann's children fill their plates with eggplant and egg rolls.

The whole thing sounds too disgusting to be true, but it is, nonetheless. Given all the trouble I've had persuading my children to eat anything that isn't plain pasta, how is that Ann's children are not only polite and brilliant, but gourmands?

"Indian children eat Indian food," she remarks after they have gone to bed (except for Ingmar, who is doing something with the computer in his father's office—probably hacking into the NSA mainframe).

"They also speak Hindi," says Christine.

"Geniuses!" I say.

We laugh, but I'm serious. In the nature versus nurture debate, here's an argument for nurture. If you feed them, they will come. The secret, Ann says, is putting healthy food in front of your children day after day and giving them options within each meal. Don't like the curried broccoli? Just eat the rice. Don't like eggplant? Just eat the tofu. Eventually their tastes will come around, and they will be stir-frying ginger before you can say Christmas in the Palouse.

Of course it all sounds so easy when Ann says it, and watching her children you'd never know they ever struggled over food. I am somewhat gratified during our last morning when the youngest, Dmitri, throws a temper tantrum because his mother put the wrong kind of jam on his bread. It's a familiar scene, repeated in households all across America (and probably India, for that matter), and it reassures me that no one is perfect, although Ann comes pretty close.

At last the jam situation is resolved, our bags are packed, and tearful farewells are said. We pile the kids and our stuff into the rental car, wave goodbye, and head down the road into Idaho. This transition between states is always difficult for Christine. She rests her forehead against the window of the car and doesn't say anything for a long time. When she does talk, she has been crying, and her voice is thick with grief.

"What's the matter?" I ask, though I already know the answer.

"I miss my family," she says.

"We haven't even seen them yet."

"I know."

But I understand what she means. Living in a place far from the people you love takes its toll on your emotional equilibrium. Sometimes the only way to survive is to erect a wall and never peek around the corner. When I met Christine in the middle of the country, she had reinvented herself as a poet, a wearer of funky dresses and red lipstick, carrying a copy of Ashbery's *Self-Portrait in a Convex Mirror*. She wanted little to do with the trees, the northern lights, and the runaway truck ramps that dot this landscape. But we never really reinvent ourselves; we just borrow a costume. Our pasts, our histories, our families—they make us who we are. Thirteen years later, as a mother herself, Christine missed her stepmother, the woman who raised her (and died when Christine was only sixteen). She missed her father's steady presence. Her cousins, uncles, aunts, and friends. She missed her home.

I squeeze her hand in the car, and we drive silently along the two-lane highway toward Orofino, Idaho, a tiny town on the banks of the Clearwater River. Lulu has fallen asleep, while Simon has been granted special dispensation to play with his Nintendo DS, given the length of our drive. The road meanders through the fields, then down a steep grade toward Lewiston, Idaho, where Christine's father lives. He will meet us in Orofino, where the family is gathering for Christmas. Lewiston is the site of a wood pulp mill, where Christine's father worked, and the entire town smells like a giant Brussels sprout (Simon thinks it smells like something worse). I shut the vent and turn on the air-conditioning as we take the cutoff for Orofino.

"Where *is* everybody?" Simon asks. It's true that the road traverses uninhabited areas, vast stretches without homes or industry. The first time Christine visited my family on Long Island, she could not fathom where one town began and the other ended. They sprawled into each other without clear delineation. Now, our children can't understand how a landscape can be empty, devoid of habitation, traffic lights, stop signs, people. Although it is beautiful, it also makes me feel lonely, and I suspect Simon is feeling the same thing.

As we snake down the Clearwater, my cell phone coverage cuts out, not to return until we leave three days later. It's an odd feeling to be in a place where cell phones do not operate, as if we have ventured into the deepest jungle or a remote desert. I can't shake the unnerving sense that someone might be trying to reach me, while realizing that anyone who truly had to track me down could do it with a little work. (It's called a landline phone.) In a world where you can't (metaphorically) reach out and touch someone, people have to (literally) reach out and touch someone to reach them. All these gadgets that bring us closer actually encourage greater distance between us. The cell phone and the BlackBerry tie us to our jobs even as they promise us an illusory freedom. If it weren't so easy to call our families, perhaps we wouldn't move so far away. If I couldn't have instant-messaged my son, perhaps I wouldn't have waited so long to come home for dinner.

In Orofino, physical visits are commonplace. During the time we spend at Christine's aunt's house, no fewer than twenty-eight different relatives drop in for a visit. At one point, there are fifteen people sleeping in three bedrooms and on the living room floor, sharing one bathroom. Instead of IMing each other, we sit around the kitchen table drinking coffee, telling tales, and rifling the refrigerator. There are Christine's four first cousins, Aunt Sue's daughters, each of whom has at least three children of her own, Christine's uncle and his new wife, and her uncle's daughter, and the daughter's son, Christine's father and his new wife, and Christine's sister, visiting from Oregon. There are various husbands, boyfriends, girlfriends, and just friends. Simon and Lulu are in kid heaven, running wild with second cousins as young as five and as old as twenty-one. For three days, I barely speak with them, except to say "Time for bed," or "Are you hungry?" or "Time for dinner." They love using the word "cousin," peppering their speech with it like some strange spice.

Christmas morning they open their presents with the rest of the children, tossing gaily striped ribbons and paper into a whirling cloud. They barely make it through the wrapping paper before they proceed to the next one. It's a veritable orgy of gift-giving: plastic toys and torn boxes litter the living room floor. The kids lie among the detritus like sated conquerors, too stuffed to focus on any individual item.

Aunt Sue sneaks outside for a smoke. Although she's been smoking most of her life, she still treats it like a surreptitious activity. I join her with a cup of coffee that's so weak it could be tea. I love Aunt Sue—love her the way I would love my own aunt. She has visited us several times in New York and Cape Cod, traveled east for our wedding, taught me secrets about gardening, canning, pickling. A high school janitor for many years, she has recently retired, focusing her energy on her prodigious garden and her extended family.

She asks me about my work, my job, the cooking. I tell her I'm frustrated with how little I can get Simon and Lulu to try. She tells me not to try so hard. "Just cook 'em dinner. If they don't eat it, that's all they're getting." She has a raspy smoker's laugh that makes me want to clear my throat for her.

From another person I would say it's not so easy, but Aunt Sue has raised four daughters and has fourteen grandchildren and two great-grandchildren. She has more experience feeding children than most "experts." We couldn't be more different—our economic backgrounds, our politics, our education—yet I understand Aunt Sue, and I think she understands me. We both love our children and dream of the best for them. But in my world, children are precious porcelain dolls, to be fussed and mussed over and treated with white gloves. Here, no one childproofs his home or worries about where the children are bicycling or makes them call home every fifteen minutes. If I were going to play amateur psychologist, I would say we give our children too much power, which makes them needy and dependent, whereas Aunt Sue gives them rules, which leads to independence.

I notice, as well, during the entirety of my visit with Aunt Sue, that there is not a single fight between siblings or parents, in contrast to my family, where everyone still seems to be struggling to find his rightful place. Her children may disagree with her, but they disagree as adults, without petty squabbling. They seem to have accomplished this without the aid of psychoanalysis or psychophar-macology. Aunt Sue may be a matriarch, but she is no tyrant.

Of course, not everything is idyllic. There are divorces and ill-nesses. There are financial problems and safety hazards. In the liv-ing room, there is a woodstove so hot it could fry a chicken. I surround it with chairs to protect the children from touching it. There are limits to my admiration.

The surest way to crowd twenty people into Aunt Sue's kitchen is to get her to promise to bake pasties. Two days after Christmas, the word goes forth, and soon spreads like gospel. Strangers pull up in their pickup trucks, revealing themselves as long-lost cousins, brothers, aunts, and just regular folk who heard what was cooking. They jumble through the doorway, ring their hearty holiday hellos, and pour themselves giant cups of weak coffee. The crowd grows, jostling for position, swapping tales of pasties late and great. You'd never know Christmas was over; at Aunt Sue's, it has never ended.

Pasties are essentially crimped pastry shells filled with meat, potatoes, and onion (although you can fill them with almost anything, and Aunt Sue always makes a vegetarian version for Christine). Because Christine's father's family immigrated from Finland, I always assumed pasties were Finnish, but they are in fact from Cornwall, England. They made it into Aunt Sue's kitchen through Amasa, Michigan, where she was born and where Finns worked the iron mines like their Cornwall cousins before them, and pasties were the portable food of choice.*

When the Cornish tin miners immigrated to America in the 1800s looking for work, they brought the pasty to the Upper Peninsula of Michigan with them. Sometimes called the Yoopie (U.P.) burrito, it became popular with other ethnic groups because it was easy to keep warm or reheat and could be eaten without utensils. It also resembled the Finnish *piiraat,* which probably hastened its ac-ceptance among the Finns.

While the men watch football and talk about hunting, the women peel, slice, and dice potatoes by hand (no fancy peelers or parers for them; they use small sharp knives). Because I neither hunt nor enjoy football, I am given special dispensation to watch the preparation, but I am specifically forbidden from helping. The men in Christine's family don't do much cooking, though the husband of one of her cousins, an Italian American, makes a mean ravioli, and the others have been known to do some grilling. It's not so much that cooking is women's work as that men are not trusted with the important things.

Christine's cousins work with assembly-line precision: Two peel, another slices, and the fourth dices. With their backs to the kitchen, they are an efficient machine; potatoes come in, and filling comes out. Aunt Sue has already prepared the dough, a simple pie crust she rolls into ovals. When the pasties are stuffed, they go into the oven to bake for forty-five minutes. No one mentions them during this time, and only Aunt Sue checks on their progress. Like so much else here, few resources are wasted second-guessing. No amount of worrying ever cooked anything.

While the pasties bake, Christine's cousins prepare an iceberg lettuce salad and slice strawberries for shortcake. Now that the smell has permeated Aunt Sue's small house, the men leave the television screen and draw closer to the kitchen. Pasties herald the New Year itself: hope, hearth, home. Here, in this house, without copper pots or bread machines, without Cuisinart, Sabatier, or Calphalon, without arugula, endive, or radicchio, a family can satisfy its hunger the good old-fashioned way: by eating.

Aunt Sue removes the pasties from the oven without fanfare, and announces dinner with the same nonchalance. In fact, the only way I know it's time to eat is when Aunt Sue asks me why I'm not. I grab a paper plate and a steaming pasty and find a place at the table.

When in Orofino, Simon and Lulu do as their cousins do. They cut into their pasties, add plenty of ketchup and some salt, and scoop the food into their mouths. The flaky pastry dissolves with the satisfying tang of hamburger and onion. For a few minutes, we are one mouth, tasting, chewing, swallowing. Linked by blood, marriage, or history, what binds us here at the table is food.

"Well?" I ask Simon.

"Good," he says.

I look to Aunt Sue, and she smiles. There is nothing in her smile but the smile itself. She could say "I told you so." But she doesn't.

I feel as if I have traveled across the country to another universe. A place where time bends, and the past and future twine into one strand of presence. Here are a few things I've learned: The more kids in a house, the easier it is to take care of them; the more miles you travel, the better the food tastes when you arrive; the more food on the table, the easier it is to get people to sit and stay for a while. We've lost something in this big busy country of ours, where restlessness, ambition, and wanderlust keep us on our feet. My resolution for the new year is to spend more time in the kitchen with my family—the immediate and the extended one.

Remember it now.

Real Cavemen Don't Eat Risotto

In the beginning, there was dinner.

Group food consumption was one of the earliest markings of human behavior. The transportation of food back to a camp differentiated humans from monkeys and apes and led to a division of labor in food gathering and preparation. So, too, the use of fire encouraged common dining, as family groups would gather to eat a shared kill. According to Peter Farb and George Armelagos in *Consuming Passions: The Anthropology of Eating*, the sharing of food led to the rise of the human family and the stability of the marital bond. They write: "Each partner to a marriage might have managed to dispense with the other for sex, for companionship, or for protection—but not for the exchange of plant and animal food."

Later, meals took on a more ritualized form, as social drinking and eating formalized ties between households and delineated servants from their masters. In Greece, women dined in separate apartments whenever guests were invited. In Rome, by contrast, according to Ian Jenkins in *Greek and Roman Life,* "No Roman thinks it embarrassing to take his wife to a dinner party." But neither women nor children were considered necessary participants at mealtime. When they did join in, they usually sat by themselves and were not permitted to recline at the table like the men.

In the Middle Ages, children were often present at the table, but were instructed to keep silent and mind their manners. In *The Babees Book* (1475), the author instructs children: "Stand until you are told to sit: keep your head, hands, and feet quiet: don't scratch yourself or lean against a post, or handle anything near. . . . If any one better than yourself comes in, retire and give your place to him. . . . Be silent while your lord drinks, not laughing, whispering, or joking." In *The Schoole of Vertue* (1557), Francis Seager writes: "Look your parents in the face, hold up your hands, and say grace before meat. Make low curtesy; wish your parents' food may do 'em good. If you are big enough, bring the food to the table. Don't fill dishes so full as to spill them on your parents' dress, or they'll be angry. . . . Let your betters sit above you. See others served first, then wait a while before eating. . . . Silence hurts no one and is fitted for a child at table."*

At the end of the nineteenth century, the shift to an industrial from an agrarian society made dining together at the end of the day more convenient for guests and family members. In many places, the noon meal was replaced by the countertop or lunchbox. Although women were no longer exiled to a back room or a separate table, children were still taught to be silent and wait until their parents were fed. In *The American Woman's Home* (1869), Catherine Beecher writes: "It is always desirable, too, to train children,

---

*These excerpts are taken from *Manners and Meals in Olden Time,* Frederick J. Furnivall, ed. (N. Trubner & Co., 1868).

when at table with grown persons, to be silent, except when addressed by others; or else their chattering will interrupt the conversation and comfort of their elders. They should always be required, too, to wait in silence, till all the older persons are helped." Etiquette guides through the 1950s have children deferring to their parents at the dinner table, and waiting for Dad to be served first.

The notion, then, that dinnertime is when parents should collect the family around the table and encourage their children to talk about what they did during the day is a very modern phenomenon, perhaps no more than fifty years old. It coincides almost precisely with the collapse of the American family. Just at the very moment when fewer of us can actually sit with our children—because of divorce, remarriage, extensive commutes, swollen real estate prices—the myth of the family meal is born. For centuries, children fared fairly well when they were ignored, fed scraps, banished—and no one asked about their homework.

This is not to condone the custom—after all, women were treated similarly, and few would argue in favor of the practice. But the assumption that dinner is an opportunity for family bonding arises only because there is so little other time to bond. If we were working together in the fields, no one would conduct a longitudinal study on the family meal. If our sons apprenticed in the family cobbler business, there would be no sociologists or politicians calling for quality time around the table. Instead, dinner would simply *be,* the thing in itself, devoid of semiotic significance. The emphasis on eating together puts all our proverbial eggs in one basket, leaving no room for mistakes, no room to breathe.

Thus we have Exploding Dad, who is so intent on *changing his life* through cooking that he cannot weather setbacks, recalcitrant children, picky eaters. He sees each shunted vegetable as an affront to his very existence, a challenge to his raison d'être. He feels that if he is going to sacrifice free time, financial stability, the brass ring on the bejeweled merry-go-round, someone should erect a statue to his perseverance. He plays high stakes poker with his own family and does not know how to bluff. He is made unhappy by the very thing intended to please him.

"They drive you crazy," says my friend Callie.

We are sitting in a Starbucks across the street from my new office, the one I rented a mere two miles from my house. If the man will not go to the city, the city will come to the man. It is my newfound hope, and New Year's resolution, to bring home the bacon from a more convenient location. Because Christine has made it clear that she doesn't like me working in the house, a local office is the next best thing. Better, even, because it has the feel of a real office, with suitemates, copiers, and fax machines, and no kitchen with a refrigerator to distract me.

Callie is a doctor, a pediatrician, who works three days a week. She tells me her kids have a menu consisting of five different meals, though none are the same as mine. Her children will eat meat loaf and lasagna, but wouldn't dream of touching pesto or burritos. "I just feed them what they want, and figure they're getting what they need," she says. She works too hard to fight with them about food. If it doesn't have sugar, or chemicals, she's willing to overlook all but the most severe taste violations.

Coming from a pediatrician, this sounds like sage advice, although I still harbor dreams of turning my children into mini-epicureans, or at least pushing their palettes into the reds and greens.

Callie laughs. "Try being a mom for more than a year," she says. "Then you'll see."

As I carry my "tall" cup of coffee across the street, I wonder if the first caveman ever worried what his children were eating. *No more grubs, Junior, until you've eaten your mastodon.* The desire to care for our young, to keep them nourished and warm, must be hardwired into our genes. The task, however, has been gender-divided, parceled out like laundry, until women have borne more than their fair share while men have become published experts at something they know so little about.

I am not a caveman. I do not eat what I kill. But there are a few things I still know how to do: light a fire, make a meal, gather the clan. Thus, with Aunt Sue as my guiding spirit, I make a pizza, preparing the dough in the bread machine (which is simplicity itself, despite its high-tech pedigree: Add ingredients in the specified order, press button, and walk away). The pizza is a big hit, with Simon having four pieces, including a special "adult" pizza made with extra garlic and black olives, and I don't even mind when Lulu complains there's a funny green thing on one of her slices (it's called oregano).

Two nights later I make shrimp with Israeli couscous. Also known as "pearl couscous" or *maftoul,* Israeli couscous differs from the better-known Moroccan variety in that it is nearly pea-sized and can be boiled like regular pasta. It has a chewier consistency and, even better, if I serve it with a little butter and salt Lulu can be coaxed into eating it. I sauté the shrimp separately in olive oil and garlic for the adults, then toss in a handful of petite peas. We eat peacefully, joyfully, and I ignore the shrimp Simon pushes to the side of his plate, silently chalking up one point for getting my children to try something new.

Later, Simon and I watch the original *Bad News Bears,* his head on my shoulder, feet curled up on my thigh. With his long hair and freckles, Simon slightly resembles Tatum O'Neal, and shares with her character the same fierce competitive spirit. We both agree the original trumps the remake, and Simon asks why every movie seems to be a remake or a sequel. I explain about the death of imagination, the economics of the film industry, and the lemming mentality of moviegoers. Despite my diatribe, he seems reasonably interested, and notes that *Toy Story 2* and *Shrek 2* are as good as, if not better than, the originals. He has a point, although I argue that their originality loses something in the second telling.

Does it get any better than this? A man, a boy, a dog, and a DVD? I love having a son with whom I can toss a baseball, watch PG movies, laugh at the same jokes, discuss the *auteur* theory of great cinema. Simon is more than just my son, my firstborn; he is my pal, and I see him blossoming into a young man before my eyes. I wish I could stop time, slow down the moment, preserve us together on this couch long enough to appreciate the short window of his childhood, etiquette manuals be damned.

"Can we rent *The Godfather*?" he asks.

"*The Godfather*?" I repeat, slightly stunned.

"It won two Academy Awards for best film."

Simon's encyclopedic knowledge sometimes amazes me, and always makes me smile. I tell him the *Godfather* movies are too violent for a nine- (nearly ten-) year-old, but perhaps we can watch them in a few years (or ten). This seems to satisfy him, and he asks if I will sit on his bed and read him a book. He takes my hand and leads me upstairs. We choose a history of the Yankees, and I read through the 1930s before we both get tired. Even though we have just spent about four hours together, he doesn't want me to leave his room. "Please, Daddy, stay," he says. I feel well loved, and slightly guilty, but I kiss him goodnight anyway, telling myself I have nothing to feel bad about. I cross the hall to Lulu's room, where she is already asleep, her blond hair matted to one cheek, arms thrown above her head. I adjust the blanket on the bed and gently kiss the top of her forehead so as not to wake her.

Downstairs, Christine is finishing cleaning the kitchen. This is another advantage of cooking dinner: I don't have to clean up. Christine and I disagree, however, about who dirties the most dishes when they cook. I subscribe to the one-pot philosophy, which explains my preference for large sauté pans, while Christine prefers many smaller pots and never met a kitchen surface she couldn't use for a cutting board. On the other hand, I like to set out my ingredients in different bowls, arranging them for ease of assembly, and I have definite views about the relative merits of different cookware, never employing just one knife when four are so much more precise.

"You really made a mess," says Christine.

"I'll clean it up," I say.

"You made dinner."

"That's okay. Go watch TV."

She looks at me as if she thinks I am being sarcastic. When she realizes I am not, she says, "We'll do it together."

I grab a dish towel and dry the pots as she washes them. I remember an old family friend whose parents refused to buy a dishwasher because they believed it a bonding experience to make their children wash and dry the dishes. Although I still think they were a little nutty, I see the virtue in requiring family members to participate in mealtime preparation and cleanup. It's the reason we insist that Simon clear the plates and Lulu set the table. Though the forks often end up where the knives should be, and food ends up on the floor, at least it teaches our children that dinner doesn't magically appear on and disappear from the table.

I wonder how many families that eat together spend more than ten minutes in the kitchen before someone rushes off to do homework, practice the piano, play a video game. Not only has the time spent preparing food decreased significantly in the last fifty years, but so has the time spent eating it, and the time spent cleaning up. These days, it's all about shoveling something into your stomach while listening to an iPod, surfing the Internet, and text-messaging with your thumbs. It's a wonder families can come to-gether at all, their perfect alignment as rare as a solar eclipse or a view of Halley's comet.

We finish cleaning, then retire upstairs, both of us exhausted from cooking, cleaning, following kids around the house. It's the end of the weekend, and I'm ready to go back to work, the easiest part of my week about to begin. I still haven't managed the jug-gling act of work and dinner, the logistical struggle of shopping, prepping, cooking, and cleaning that seems to swallow half a day. There's a reason men hunted and women gathered, and it had less to do with sexism than with a reasonable division of labor. When the jobs get jumbled, parents get fried, and children bear the un-happy consequences.

By Thursday, however, it's my turn again. I come home early from my office with grandiose plans. "Risotto," I announce, which triggers howls of protest that I ignore by banishing the children to watch television (a punishment almost as bad as forcing them to eat candy). Once upon a time, Simon loved risotto. At two, he would eat it with mushrooms or beets, asparagus or peas. Perhaps he confused it with oatmeal, or rice pudding, but in any event, he was hooked. Then he grew weary of strange foods with odd ingre-dients, and insisted that all his food be white or beige. Soon, he forgot he had ever liked risotto, or ever ate it. Until Thursday night. That's when, despite his protests, Simon tried risotto again, prodded (he might say "goaded") by his father. Better yet, he liked it. Perhaps "liked" is too strong a word—"tolerated" might be more accurate. But let's not get picky! After five months of cook-ing, my son is officially willing to take chances on foodstuffs. Maybe it's my culinary prowess, maybe it's wanting to please Dad, maybe he's just hit the right age. But whatever the cause, although he picked through the onions, he still put the risotto in his mouth, and chewed, and swallowed, and seemed to be eating it.

Lulu, on the other hand, was a different story. How a child who likes basmati and sushi rice can dislike risotto remains one of the great mysteries of the new millennium. Creamy and bland (unless you use a sharp Parmesan cheese, which I did not), it should appeal to simple palates. Of course, the simple palates must put it in their mouths first, which Lulu refused to do. You can't know you hate it unless you've tried it. But I've given up singing that song.

Both children went to bed without any snacks, even though Lulu complained she was hungry. Her pleas, however, failed to move me. No child of which I am aware has ever successfully completed a hunger strike. In some cultures, children actually eat first, then ask questions later. I may not be able to persuade my children to eat my food, but I can put it on the table, offer them a taste, then send them to bed without screaming at them. That is progress.

But it is short-lived. Not through any fault of theirs, but through my own limitations in the kitchen.

I may not be a caveman, but I am also not a gourmet chef. I lack the skills of even the most basic Culinary Arts graduate. Though I worked in a restaurant for many years, I spent exactly one night in the kitchen, where I promptly burned my hand on a baked stuffed lobster and had to receive emergency medical treatment. Over the years I have picked up certain tricks (smash iceberg lettuce on its stem to de-core it; cross-hatch an onion before slicing to dice it; drop a tomato in boiling water to remove its skin), but none would get me my own TV show (though some have gotten me a second date). Sometimes inspiration strikes; other times, it strikes out.

This meal should have been a surefire winner: baked stuffed potatoes and scrod (a bland, totally inoffensive fish). Instead, it was gross. Maybe it was the sour cream in the potatoes, which has never been one of my favorites, or the fish, which tasted undercooked and slimy. Though Christine said she liked the fish, and Simon and Lulu tried the potatoes, I thought it was unpalatable. Which just goes to show: There's no accounting for taste. Or, one man's scrod is another man's gelatinous, undersalted, coconutty mess.

But here's what I really want to remember from this meal, which was otherwise forgettable: When I asked Simon if he wanted some fish, he took a deep breath, and then said, "Okay, I'll try some," steeling himself for the new experience rather than rejecting it outright. His bravery in the face of such overwhelming odds was nothing short of heroic.

Mealtime has evolved since the days the first caveman dragged the first carcass across the steppe. For one thing, the food is easier to kill. It's also easier to abdicate responsibility for it, leaving dinner to neither the hunters nor the gatherers but the take-outers.* We can never go back to those heady days when women served, children were scarce, and men banged the table with the blunt handles of their knives. Yet why would we want to? Yes, we live in a complicated world, where we take our families as we find them, sometimes in prescheduled packages between station breaks. It's the way we live now, and what's been lost in translation is more than just words.

But as I sit down on my son's bed and feel his warm breath against my cheek, I realize there's no earthly reason I wouldn't want to share my dinner with him. It strikes me that we've had it

*Thus the joke: What does Dad make for dinner? Reservations.

wrong all these years. Children are meant to be present at the table as active participants—not because some child psychologist has ordained that it's good for them, or increases their self-esteem, or improves our share of "quality time," but because amid the jangle and disorder of dinner there are tucked away moments of sheer bliss, when your son will raise a piece of fish to his lips, close his eyes, and take a chance, sharing in the most primordial of urges and making you feel, despite the setbacks, drawbacks, and blow-backs, profoundly and unabashedly happy.

That's My Nest Egg You're Stepping On

If all happy families eat, drink, and are merry, unhappy families must be hungry.

"What are you doing here?" asks Christine.

I am, in fact, chopping vegetables for a stir-fry. It is four o'clock on a Wednesday afternoon. Lulu is at gymnastics, and Simon is with a friend. When Christine arrives with her laptop and a shopping bag, her face falls at the sight of me happily slicing and listening to music.

"I thought you were at work."

"I was," I explain. "Then I came home."

"But don't you have to work?"

"I have to make dinner."

This doesn't seem to satisfy her, and she frowns deeply as she unpacks the contents of her bag.

"Is something the matter?" I ask, my tone implying nothing should be.

"It's too much togetherness," she says.

"Too much togetherness?"

"I thought you were going to work in your office."

"I *was* working. Now I'm cooking."

"But it's four o'clock."

"When am I supposed to chop the vegetables?"

"I don't know. It's not that. It's just that you seem to be home a lot lately."

"Wasn't that the point?"

Christine frowns again, but doesn't say anything. This is part of a simmering, and recent, argument between us, and an unintended consequence of Dinner with Dad. It began in the fall, when she objected to my working in the house, saying that it disrupted her routine. But now that I've rented a local office, the argument has expanded to include my unwelcome and surprise presence at random hours of the day. Yesterday, for example, she was upset to find me home at lunch making a turkey sandwich. Although I had just returned for half an hour, it coincided with the time she planned to take the dog for a walk, and that led to a heated discussion about whether the dog should be left to roam free in the backyard or cooped up in the house.

"I love you, Cameron," says Christine, beginning a sentence that inevitably follows with *but*. "But you're a hard person to be around."

This, too, is not a new argument, although it has taken on new urgency in recent months. Have I always been "a hard person to be around"? It seems to me I have grown more brittle with age, my patience a thin veneer easily scratched. I believe closets should be organized and phone calls returned promptly. I do not understand why the soap can't go back to its own dish or the cap screwed onto the toothpaste tube. I'm not a tyrant, exactly, but even in high school my girlfriend used to call me "Correct Cam," for my insistence on being right all the time. Over the years, my natural ten-

dency to control things has become more pronounced, growing in
inverse proportion to my ability to control them. The only saving
grace, from Christine's perspective, has been my absence. With little time available to complain, Christine survived my occasional
harangues by ignoring them.

Now, however, it's All Cam All the Time. In the mornings,
I question whether the kids should be eating sugary cereal or
Go-Gurt. At lunch, I ask why the mail has not yet been picked up.
Before dinner, I want to know why the dishwasher hasn't been
emptied.

"I'm just asking," I say.

"It's annoying," says Christine. "I feel like you're constantly
monitoring me."

But isn't that what marriage is all about? In sickness and in
health, for better or for worse, on videotape and webcam.

"But not for lunch," says Christine.

This seems unreasonable to me. When Lulu returns home,
she is excited to see me, and wants to help chop the vegetables. We
select a song from my iPod and dance around the kitchen to the
Pussycat Dolls. I even convince her to eat a sugar snap pea, although she refuses to eat the sweet husk, splitting it open instead
to eat the tiny peas inside. I ignore this minor transgression because I am in my element, preparing food, listening to music, and
shaking my bootie with my oh-so-hip daughter. Why shouldn't
Christine share my joy?

Instead, she retreats into her office, where she works on the
novel she has been writing for five or six years.

"Where's Mommy?" Lulu asks.

"Stewing," I say.

But when she emerges for dinner, Christine is in a perfectly
fine mood. She doesn't carry a grudge, which makes her a better
person than me. It certainly makes her easier to live with.

The next day, however, she finds me sweaty and stretched out on the living room carpet. I've just come back from a five-mile run, and I plan to return to my office after showering. It's not as if I'm not working; I'm just taking a long lunch break—no longer, really, than what I might take if I went to lunch with a client. But Christine doesn't see it that way.

"I don't understand. What happened to your job?"

"Nothing happened. I'm teaching three days a week, and working in Westport two days a week."

"Then why are you here?"

"I live here, remember?"

Christine bites her lip and turns to leave the room.

"Are you telling me I can't come back to my own house?" I ask.

She takes a breath. Then she says, "I wish you could have a normal job and leave the house in the morning at eight and come home at six."

"But then I wouldn't be able to make dinner."

"You could make it on the weekend."

"But that's not the point." It disturbs me that Christine fails to understand the Dinner with Dad premise. I feel like Albert Brooks in *Lost in America*, explaining the concept of a "nest egg." Why work so hard if my wife undermines the very purpose of the endeavor?

"I get it," she says. "I just didn't think you'd be home all the time."

"It's not 'all the time.' I'm going back to my office as soon as I shower."

And so on. We fight for about twenty minutes, until I wear her down, which is my usual strategy. She doesn't give in so much as give out, tiring of the back-and-forth, the skills I have honed over eighteen years of litigating, until she concedes she has over-reacted and I am welcome in the house any time I choose. It's not a fair fight, really, but it doesn't leave me feeling victorious, just unsettled. Even as I argue Christine into submission, I realize I can't win her heart with logic and righteous indignation. These are, in fact, the very things that make her reluctant to have me around.

Could it be that in trying to change my life I have accentuated the flaws I was trying to change? Before I started making dinner I was impatient, moody, and unavailable. Now I am impatient, moody, and available. At least when everyone was asleep, no one had to bear my constant criticism (except the dog). Now I have hours to complain that the carrot peeler has been moved from its usual spot in the top drawer to some undetermined location.

Even the children have not escaped my watchful eye. While Simon used to do his homework in relative peace, now I hover over him, checking his calculations and punctuation. It annoys me that he misses simple arithmetic problems, sums that I know he is capable of computing if only he would pay better attention. His sloppy handwriting drives me crazy—the way he scrawls his answers in unregimented lines so they bleed over the page, then crosses out words until the result is an unmitigated and unreadable glop. We get into shouting matches, as if he were a truculent teenager instead of a boy who has yet to reach double digits, and I send him to bed without any TV.

Instead of exercising patience with my daughter, her whining sets my teeth on edge, like nails across a blackboard. When she spills water at the table I take her to task for her clumsiness. When she leaves her markers uncapped, I make a show of tossing them into the garbage, even though they could probably be revived with a little water and a good recapping. I buy her a three-dollar bracelet, which she loses, and I give her a stern lecture about treating gifts with respect.

I am, in short, the father of my nightmares. Who would want

me around? Better to stay in Grand Central Terminal eating a taco in a windowless warren and sneaking back home after dark. Which is what I do for the next two nights, feeling sorry for myself rather than distressed by my behavior. If my wife refuses to grasp how lucky she is that her husband cooks for her, I will punish her by not cooking. If my children do not appreciate a father who keeps them on the straight and narrow, I will let their deviancies grow unchecked. Let them eat cake, or fried chicken nuggets.

On the third morning, however, Lulu comes downstairs as I am packing my laptop. "Daddy," she says, "did you go to Kansas?"

In fact, I have been sleeping upstairs, forty feet away from her. But I realize that when she doesn't see me, I might as well be in Kansas. I explain I have been working late, but it feels like a lie. If I'd wanted to, I know I could have come home earlier. My actions suddenly strike me as childish and immature, not the conduct of a grown man, a father of two, a husband of thirteen years. As Christine has often pointed out, I overreact rather than react. My wife has not banished me from the house; she has merely expressed her feelings about my erratic schedule, feelings that I later learn are not uncommon. My friend Callie, for example, says she can hardly wait for Monday after spending the weekend with her husband. "It's not that I don't love him," she explains. "It's just that we have our schedule, and weekends are hard."

Most of the women with whom I feel comfortable discussing the situation agree: It's easier when their husbands are not around. One friend tells me she prefers it when her husband travels. "It's the best of both worlds," she says. "When he comes home I've really missed him." When I post an entry on my blog about the issue, the responses are uniformly sympathetic to the struggles of the stay-at-home parent whose routine is interrupted by the well-meaning, if intrusive, working parent (with the exception of a post from a twenty-year-old college student, who insists marriage should be bliss). One reader writes about the six-month trauma of sharing the house with her husband when he was out of work. Another recounts the tragic tale of converting a spare bedroom into a home office, resulting in no room for guests or for herself.*

For every wife who thinks mine is fortunate to have a husband who actually wants to cook, there is another who grimaces (or the online equivalent) at the mere suggestion. One writes: "My husband barbecues. Period. I wouldn't let him near the kitchen." Men are messy, bossy, and always take too much credit for the simplest things. *Look, Ma, I made a mud pie!* There's hunting, and gathering, and emptying the dishwasher. Only a fool, or a braggart, would try to do it all.

Among our friends, when the husband cooks it's an activity restricted to weekends or special occasions. Even when both parents are working, dinner falls to mom. Dad can be entrusted with a slab of beef, but not much more. Although one working mother I know complains her husband is never home for dinner, in the same breath she says she enjoys the time to focus on her children at the end of her day. Another mother notes on a UC Berkeley message board that women unconsciously (subconsciously? consciously?) "claim the house as their domain, relegating their husbands to a sort of incompetent guest visitor status," then complain

---

By contrast, on one popular website devoted to griping mothers—urbanbaby .com—the message boards overflow with postings about absent husbands. "Unf**king believable!!!" writes one. "DH [dear husband] comes home, eats dinner w/ us, then goes upstairs and I find he's doing his keyboard. His excuse, well I had dinner w/ you." In fact, the number one complaint from wives about their husbands is that they don't contribute enough to household chores and parenting duties. As one wife put it in *Newsday*, criticizing her husband's failure to help around the house: "He has perfected the husbandly art of playing stupid. I don't know where they learn it, but they all do it."

when they don't take enough responsibility for parenting and household decisions.

"Why do you think people get divorced after they retire?" Callie asks.

I never understood why couples would wait until the twilight of their lives to split, yet I know two couples who have done so in the last year. Apparently, the strain of spending too much time together takes its toll. *Too much togetherness.* If human beings were meant to mate for life, they were never intended to work at home. It's why libraries, reading groups, and shuffleboard were invented.

Two problems confront me, however. The first is how to survive thirty more years of marriage without becoming a shuffleboard addict. The second is how to continue making dinner while not being strangled by my wife. Although I still think her unreasonable, in the light of the morning, freshly caffeinated, I can see how a husband puttering around in the kitchen could be disruptive. Especially if that husband tends to have strong feelings about where the spatulas should be housed.

Now my sloe-eyed daughter regards me watchfully. For her, I put on some black beans to boil and make the crowd-pleasing favorite: black bean burritos (with garlic shrimp for the adults). For one meal we have no complaints, my wife is happy to have me home, and no one goes to sleep hungry. The next night, however, I try to make pasties, following Aunt Sue's recipe but with disastrous results. The problem arises when I make the mistake of a novice cook, substituting butter for lard. Little did I know that rendered pig fat is what gives pie crust its flaky quality. (Aunt Sue uses Crisco, which I avoid because it contains hydrogenated vegetable oil, the evil ingredient du jour.) As a result, although my filling resembles Aunt Sue's, my crust is dry and crumbly. Christine claims to enjoy the vegetarian pasty I've made for her, but neither Simon nor Lulu will take more than a bite. In an instant, I become Bad Dad, as angry at myself for screwing up the recipe as I am at them for not humoring me. They go to sleep hungry, and I go to my office where I surf the Internet for an hour reading about perfect piecrusts.

Later, lying awake in my bed, I wonder whether being a father has really made me a better person. Before I had children, my friends always insisted that being a parent taught patience, responsibility, perspicacity. They suggested (at least implicitly) that people without children were immature, naïve, selfish, or just plain stupid. Some of this, I knew, was the self-congratulatory and self-preserving tendency of anyone who has chosen a particular path—career, marriage, or child-rearing.* We pride ourselves on the choices we've made so as not to despair over the alternatives (although, of course, sometimes despair wins, leading to divorce, job-hopping, etc.). But I also think we truly believe our own propaganda: The struggles over bedtime, TV watching, computer use, friends, camp, cars, girls, boys, make us better people. That which does not kill me makes me stronger.

But as I toss and turn, I wonder whether any of these sacred platitudes are valid. Sometimes, in fact, I think just the opposite is true: Having children makes us impatient, immature, impulsive, and unwise. Trying to convince my son that a piecrust made with butter is the functional equivalent of one made with Crisco, and then getting angry when he refuses to accept my logic, is not the sign of a wise or patient man. If my (childless) brother were sitting at the table, I know he would not yell at Simon, but would deal with his refusal to eat a pasty in a calm and adult manner. Having to confront the defiance of children daily, however, has made me

---

* When I was single, every one of my married friends wanted to know when I was getting married, as if they couldn't bear to be alone.

edgy and easily provoked. Worse, it has increased my need for "alone" time and, if anything, made me more selfish about getting it. While I understand rationally that children can behave irrationally, I'm not sure it has made me any better equipped to deal with irrationality. In fact, rather than finding it charming, amusing, or mildly frustrating, my children's recalcitrance drives me batty.

The arguments in favor of parenting strike me, in the end, as nothing more than elaborate rationalizations for an absurd act: having children. I haven't chosen to propagate out of some sense that it will make me better, stronger, faster, wiser, or able to leap tall buildings in a single bound; just the opposite, as my aching back confirms. Absurdity cannot be justified, or even explained. It just is. Love is an absurd act. None of us choose it, and we certainly don't love because we think it will lower our cholesterol or whiten our teeth. It is irrational, ineffable, at times insufferable. But when it climbs on our lap at the end of a hard day and clips a pair of sparkly earrings to our ears, we know we wouldn't want it any other way.

Three A.M. My daughter cries out in her sleep. I get up and pad to her room, but she has resumed sleeping soundly. I go downstairs, where Sugar greets me happily, licking my hand as if I've just brought her candy instead of waking her in the middle of the night. I pour myself a glass of water and sit at the kitchen table. Sugar curls back up at my feet.

Six months ago I was unhappy, overworked, and missed my family. How much has changed? For one thing, I see my family so much that my wife needs a break. Overworked? If anything, my working day has shrunk to the bare minimum. With almost no law to practice, and only my teaching and writing, there are more hours in the week available to sleep than to work. Unhappy? That is the more difficult question. My unhappiness has taken a differ-

ent form. Where once I felt overwhelmed, now I feel unappreciated. Where once I felt alienated, now I feel smothered. My life
has improved because I have been more involved in my children's
activities, but with that involvement has come disappointment,
disagreement, and conflict. Where once I imagined I would whisk
into my family's life, bringing laughter, joy, and good food, I now
realize it's more complicated than that. My presence itself is a dis-
traction, and not always a good one. My Type A behavior has
made me poorly suited to the chaos of child-rearing. My glass jaw
and tin ear have made me a bad companion for my wife. Sometimes it's better to have a warm and fuzzy picture of Dad than the
angry corporeal reality.*

And yet I'm trying, God help me, I'm really trying. If the alternative is to go back to the way it was, that's no choice at all. I
haven't flunked the Dad Test—not yet, not ever. I'm still standing,
and still cooking. I haven't microwaved anything yet.

Sugar nudges my ankle. *Stop worrying,* she says. *Shut off the
light and let me lie here in peace.*

I pat her on the head and let her lick my hand again. "It'll be
okay, Sugar," I say, to myself really, if not to her. Then I switch off
the lights and go back upstairs to bed.

---

*One of my blog posters notes how she couldn't wait to stop having dinner with
her father because of his tyrannical nature. Dinner was an opportunity for him
to harass and bully her, and she was glad to be freed of it.

The Root
Vegetable of
All Evil

And then the second boot falls. On my neck.

For the first time in a long while, we are short on our monthly expenses. To pay our mortgage, I write a check from our home equity line of credit. It is a big check. We have a large mortgage.

I spend the rest of the day in a state of mounting panic. I knew this day was coming, but I didn't think it would arrive so soon, so fast, so hard. I make some quick calculations and realize that although we can survive off our home equity until the end of the year, eventually we will drain our funds and end up deeply in debt.

How did I get here? My decision to stop traveling to Kansas, to cut back on work, to leave the office at a reasonable hour and come home for dinner. A man can't sit down at the table with his family five nights a week by working eighty hours in his office. But eighty hours a week is what has sustained us in this expensive part of the country for many years. Unless I am prepared to overcome my wife's objections, my children's unhappiness, my parents' dismay, and my siblings' distress and move us to a place where the cost of living is cheaper, I have to find a better way to balance the family budget.

This, of course, is easier said than done. With various expenses looming (insurance, camp, cars, etc.), the boot came crashing down on Saturday night when I tried to make spaghetti with vegetarian meatballs. I couldn't find a suitable meat substitute, and the one I did find was meant for tacos. Christine pointed this out, and I stormed from the house, railing about vegetarians, to buy some hamburger meat. When I returned, everyone had eaten, and I made spaghetti and real meatballs for one. I ate my dinner alone at the kitchen table while the kids took a bath, Christine read them stories, and they went to sleep.

Happy?

Money isn't everything, it's true. It can't buy love, and it doesn't buy happiness.* The inability to pay my mortgage without borrowing, however, is sobering and disquieting. I am not without options, and far from homeless. Unlike many other people in my situation, I actually have assets that, in a pinch, I could sell. I have parents to whom I could turn, and siblings that would always take me in. I will never starve. But as anyone who hasn't been able to pay the bills understands, the brush with financial insolvency is a soul-shaking experience. It starts as a low thrum, a steady beat that mounts gradually into the hum of a full-fledged panic. It is different from the poverty of a graduate student, shaking pockets for spare change for pizza. Back then the situation felt both temporary and romantic, the lot of the young writer (or law student), soon to be alleviated by the sale of the Great American Novel (or

---

*According to economist Robert H. Frank, studies show that the average level of happiness remains unchanged even in countries that experience a substantial growth in income. Indeed, people who focus intently on material success have low levels of happiness.

the ridiculously overpaid big-firm salary). Now, however, not only does the future look bleak, but there are three other people relying on me to pay the bills.

I lie awake while Christine sleeps soundly next to me, running various scenarios through my brain. Why not leave New York? What is keeping me here? We live in one of the most expensive housing pockets in the country, with high taxes and outrageous charges for everything from parking permits to babysitters.* We joke that hiring anyone to do something around the house automatically results in a 30 percent markup because of our location, which is probably not far from the truth. Throwing a birthday party at a bowling alley costs more than most people spend on food in a month. Parking a car in Manhattan can set us back as much as a hotel room in Idaho. The monthly rail commute is more expensive than a car payment. For the price of sending our children to day camp, we could send them to private school in Kansas. A trip to the supermarket feels like shopping on Rodeo Drive.

I fall asleep and have an anxiety dream in which I am arrested for a crime I did not know I committed, and for which I do not have an alibi. As I am led away in handcuffs, protesting my innocence, I see my children cozying up to a man who looks suspiciously like my wife's college boyfriend. I wake up in a cold sweat.

I begin to notice the cost of everything as I commute to work. While I never thought twice about buying the newspaper at the train station, it now strikes me as an unnecessary expense because I can usually pick one up when someone else has finished reading. I realize I spend at least five hundred dollars a year at Starbucks. Lunch costs a small fortune, since I never bring my own. Ridicu-

---

* Between 2000 and 2004, according to *The New York Times,* property taxes grew two to three times faster than personal income in the New York metropolitan region.

lous things infuriate me, like the two seventy-nine I have to pay for six Advil at Grand Central, or the dollar eighty for a bottle of water (water!), which is essentially a by-product of the soda manufacturing process. The more I calculate, the more my panic grows, along with the sense that I have lost control of my future, that my grand experiment is doomed to failure because of something as simple and basic as a job.

Like a drug addict, however, I keep my secrets to myself. I move money around from home equity to bank account to credit card. Instead of sharing my woes with Christine, I get angry about small expenses, like the sports bottles she buys for the kids. Why do our children need another container for drinking when they already have three or five and have lost a dozen? Christine ignores me, as is her wont, and the kids are too busy racing around the house with Sugar to notice. By bedtime, I've calmed down, enough so that I can read each child a book and not wonder why we can't use the library rather than Barnes & Noble.

But at night the panic returns. I don't sleep well. I get up at three, again at four, and for good at five. It's the first time in my life I feel my finances slipping away from me, out of my control, and I'm unable to pull some trick out of my wallet. I've always been pretty good about making money, finding a way to cash out when I needed to, which probably explains why I haven't fully considered the consequences of giving up work to come home for dinner. I've assumed things would work out, as they always have, with a new job, or a bonus, or the sale of a book or an article. But now, with no relief in sight, it dawns on me that I am headed toward financial calamity.

I consider asking my parents for a loan, but since my wounds are self-inflicted, I cannot bring myself to do it. It was my choice to slow down, to give up the income that sustained us in the style to which we had become accustomed. I'm also not sure how sympathetic my parents will be, since they've made it clear they don't approve of where we live, even though housing costs across the region are similar. My father survived on his academic salary, and I should be able to, too. It would do no good to point out that the house he bought for $68,000 could not be purchased for less than a million dollars today. Or that my college tuition was less than my son's camp.

No one has forced my choices upon me, however, unpalatable as they may be. My situation is more complicated, but no different really, than that of plenty of working parents. The trade-off between family time and work is made by many people every day. Few of us feel we have a choice, but many of us do without actually admitting it: The banker who never puts his kids on the bus, the lawyer who never sees a school play, the businesswoman who is always traveling. These are not people without choices. I am reminded of this as I read Eugene O'Kelly's memoir *Chasing Daylight*. The former CEO of accounting giant KPMG, O'Kelly was diagnosed with terminal brain cancer in May 2005, when he was fifty-three years old. Told he had no more than six months to live, he set himself the task of embracing his death with the same rigor and energy as he had embraced his work.

Though the book is remarkable—lucid, painful, and heartbreaking—what strikes me is that O'Kelly had lived most of his working life without coming to the realizations that only his impending death made possible. This was a guy who once flew twenty-two hours to Australia in order to woo a client on a connecting shuttle flight of ninety minutes, and then turned around and flew twenty-two hours home. He worked all the time, and appeared to have little time for his family. By his own admission, the only vacations he took with his wife and daughter were those that involved work conferences, and the only free time he seemed to have were golf outings with business buddies (and occasionally his wife). Three months after he realized his life was out of balance, he died.

I wonder how many meals O'Kelly managed to share with his entire family (and not just with his wife on a business trip) before he couldn't stomach real food anymore? How many rungs on the corporate ladder would he have sacrificed if he could have eaten just a few more? I admire O'Kelly for coming to terms with his death. It's his life that leaves something to be desired. You can't work around the clock, travel the world, spend no time with your family, and then make it right in three months. How does his fourteen-year-old daughter feel now that her father is gone, and the best time she got to spend with him was during the three months when he finally slowed down? Does it compensate for the years he was flying to business meetings or out on the golf course? O'Kelly may have realized his life was out of balance, but the real sadness of the book is that it was too little, too late.

It seems to me the world is divided into two kinds of people: those who sympathize with the man bent on changing his life, and those who think he should get over it.

In my case, the former are mostly friends who live the same kind of high-maintenance lifestyle I do. They nod empathetically at how hard it is to have time and money for everything, to be a good father and good provider while still getting home in time to coach baseball and basketball and put a meal on the table. "I don't know how you do it," they say, which would be a good title for a book if Allison Pearson hadn't already nabbed it. They tell me they admire my efforts, then ask me not to say anything to their wives. Or, if they are women, they insist I have a talk with their husbands. I smile, shrug politely, and say it's not as easy as it seems. Of course not; nothing worth doing ever is. Then they finish their four-dollar coffee and drive off in their $45,000 Lexus with the Nantucket sticker on the rear.

The latter are best represented by another reader of my blog who writes: "GET THE HECK OUT OF NYC!" It's a loser's game, he says. The only way to win is not to play.

Like Eugene O'Kelly, it is somewhat duplicitous to live a certain way, then seek sympathy when your own choices cause you pain. But, unlike O'Kelly, I hope I have more than three months (God willing) to change my life. Make a list, I tell myself; what do you value? High-powered New York suburbs? Then forget about seeing your kids for dinner five days a week. Laid-back free-range lifestyle with woodstove and flannel sheets? Then say goodbye to your parents, your siblings, the teaching job you love. You can't have everything. Where would you put it?

In the midst of this navel-gazing, I cook as though my life depends upon it, which perhaps it does. Shrimp scampi, white chili, raclette. But each effort results in failure, as if my children are calling my bluff. If you're trying to change your life by making dinner, they say, forget about it. At the end of the day, you'll be poor, hungry, and searching for Tupperware. But you won't be any closer to salvation.

It's just dinner, after all. It's not a cure for cancer or heart disease or diabetes. It won't turn mere mortals into Tour de France champions. It's not even likely to earn a spot on the Food Network. You can cook, but you can't hide: from your obligations, your commitments, your cable television bill.

I begin to make phone calls to former colleagues, old bosses, lawyers with whom I've worked. I go for an interview with a headhunter. We have an animated ninety-minute discussion, and she concludes that I am lost, wandering, searching for the stones I've left in the woods to light my way. Sympathy, yes; work, no.

This is ridiculous, I say to Christine, finally owning up to my financial despair, I don't have to continue. I could stop making dinner tomorrow and get a normal job at a law firm. Become the kind of lawyer I wrote about in *Double Billing:* unhappy, under-trained, overworked, mistreated, unappreciated, doing the devil's work.

"How do you really feel about it?" she asks.

But even if I could get a law firm job, which I doubt, I am not a quitter. Despite the headhunter's words, I don't feel lost; in fact, I have never been clearer about my ambitions: to change the world, one mouth at a time.

"What's the worst that could happen?" Christine asks me. "Be realistic. Will we have to sell our house?"

"No," I say.

"Will the kids have to leave their school?"

"No."

"Then what?"

"We could owe a lot of money on our home equity loan."

"You said you would do it for a year, right?"

"The *school year,*" I remind her.

"It's three more months."

"Four."

"We'll manage."

If either of us recognizes this role reversal, we don't acknowledge it. Instead, I ask, "And after that, what?"

There are two kinds of people in the world: Those who think the sky is falling, and those who buy hats. I do not own a hat.

"One day at a time," says Christine.

And so, like recovering workaholics, we put on our blinders and vow not to think about tomorrow. At least not while today still burns brightly and we have our health and our children. Knock on wood.

Instead, like most Americans stretched to their limits, we go on vacation.

Normally, this would be the worst thing in the world, the last thing I need in my depleted financial state. The airplane tickets to Los Angeles, however, have already been paid for seven months earlier, as have the hotel room and the tickets to Universal Studios. The trip, therefore, is not quite free, but it feels that way, since it's coming from pre–Dinner with Dad funds. The rest of our activities—walking in Venice, sightseeing on Hollywood Boulevard, visiting old friends—are freebies. It is also our first real vacation in several years, the first time we've gone somewhere that wasn't to visit family or attend a bar mitzvah or a wedding.

I think about Eugene O'Kelly as we board the Jet Blue flight to Long Beach. He dreamed about traveling to Europe with his daughter before he died, but he never got the chance. Instead, the cancer spread, and he grew too weak and then too feeble to care for himself. In the end, his wife had to finish his book.

I vow not to do that to my wife.

Christine is a terrible air traveler. White-knuckled, pale-faced, and rigid with fear. She grips the armrests as if willing the plane to stay in the air. But when we land, all is forgiven. The sunny California clime greets us like an old friend. We rent a convertible, put the top down, and drive north on the interstate singing Beach Boys songs. In Santa Monica, the concierge takes our bags and encourages us to walk along the pier. Lulu runs ahead with Simon in hot pursuit, and Christine and I hold hands like a newlywed couple.

In this year of making dinner, I realize, there has been little time to relax. Instead, I've traded one form of stress for another. The anxiety of working too much has given way to the anxiety of working too little, the tension of coming home on time replaced by the tension of being home too much of the time. But riding a roller coaster with a nine-year-old boy puts everything in perspective. As Simon makes me go back on the Revenge of the Mummy for the third time, I understand that the family vacation (or "fake-ation," as a friend calls it) is not necessarily about being pampered, or playing nine holes of golf, but about connecting with family members whose daily drumbeats go mostly unnoticed by working dads (and moms). Traveling together, eating together, shopping together, sleeping together, there's a rhythm that is usually missing from the workaday world. Vacations differ even from weekends because the kids are not running off to their baseball games, soccer matches, birthday parties, etc. Instead, it is family—24/7.

The roller coaster whips forward, then stops, trembles, and begins to accelerate backward. Terrifying dips and drops are replaced by hair-raising twists and head-spinning turns. Simon laughs with abandon while I grab the safety bar like a nervous flyer. Whose idea was this, I wonder. And when can I get off?

"Let's go again!" says Simon when the ride ends.

"Again?" I ask.

"*Da*-ad," he says, as if he can't believe how dense I am. Who wouldn't want to ride this wild roller coaster with the crazy ups and downs, the sickening feeling of the ground giving way beneath your feet, the contents of your stomach churning like butter or battery acid?

"Bring it on," I say.

The smile on his face is broad enough to swallow the moon.

Miles to Go
Before I Eat

Once upon a time, running was what I did. Seven days a week, 365 days a year, through all weather and at all hours. I ran in the middle of a twenty-two-inch snowstorm in New York City, venturing into Central Park when the roads were impassable to cars. I ran in Iowa when it was three degrees—minus twenty with the wind chill—my fingers so cold I couldn't straighten them completely for days afterward. I ran through midtown Manhattan when it was so hot the pavement literally melted and my shoes stuck to the hot tar. As a young lawyer, I ran home alone through Central Park at ten or eleven at night, trotting around the northern end of the park with the streetlights broken and frightening shadows lurking in the woods. When I worked at CBS, my secretary thought I was having an affair because I disappeared nearly every day at lunch to go to the gym. In Yugoslavia I left my girlfriend alone in a hotel to jog down roads so narrow I was nearly killed by passing motorists. In Italy, traveling with my wife, too sick to go out for New Year's Eve, I found enough energy to run, stopping only to vomit beside the river before continuing back to my hotel. I ran a race the day before our wedding (setting a course record) and another on our honeymoon in Santa Fe (nearly passing out from the altitude). I ran a race at four in the morning and another one at midnight. I ran races that took twenty-four hours, covered distances from 400 meters to 186 miles, required teams of two to twelve people. Even after my children were born, I ran as though I had something to fear, taking them with me in the baby jogger, or simply insisting on time to exercise. *Getting in my run* was like a mantra; I built my entire day around it. Nothing stopped me, until my Achilles tendon popped and my hamstrings just up and quit, victims of too many miles and too many hills. Even then, I ran until blood pooled in my calves, the flesh swelling a sickly yellow color, spongy and hot to the touch.

Given my lifelong devotion to (some would say obsession with) running, how can I let a little thing like dinner defeat me? I have never dropped out of a race, never quit in the middle of a workout, never given up while I still had strength to stand. It hasn't always been easy, and it certainly hasn't been pretty, but running has literally carried me through some of the darker times.*

Although they might appear to be different, running and cooking have many things in common. Perspiration, not inspiration, is the rule. The ratio of bad days to good is about seven to one. Both are a means to an end, yet the end is rarely the goal. Instead, the finish line is a constantly moving target, each day a step

---

* When I lived in Washington, D.C., I went running with a colleague who had just broken up with his long-term girlfriend, which I didn't know until he burst into tears in the middle of our run. When I suggested we stop, he insisted we pick up the pace, until we were practically flying down the Mall, leaving tourists and his sadness in our wake.

toward the next, each race a progression in a lifelong pursuit of speed, fitness, and endorphins.

When I first began running, in my early teens, I ran to win. When I lost, I contemplated quitting, and sometimes did— although I always returned to the sport. But something happened along the way, sometime after I graduated from college and imagined I would give up running once and for all. I discovered I was hooked—not on the experience of winning (although there's nothing like crossing the tape, arms aloft, chest extended, trophy anticipated), but to running itself. I loved the feeling of freedom I had out on the roads, the sense of my body working hard, of being in tune with the environment and at peace with the world. I never ran with a Walkman (or, later, an iPod), but used the time purely contemplatively, an opportunity to hear the world around me or to let my mind wander on whatever course it would travel. Though the runs got harder as I got older, and many were physically painful, I never finished without being glad I had run. A bad day running beat just about anything else.

When we return from Los Angeles, I go for a run after the kids are in bed and the roads are dark and cold. What is it about running that makes me so determined to do it, no matter the time, conditions, or conflicts? In part, I have become a running addict, dependent on the "fix" of chemicals that flood my brain after every run. But it is also, I realize, an ordering of priorities, a determination of what is important to me and a refusal to let distractions interfere with it.

Running is something I cannot *not* do—at least when I am physically able. It helps that I enjoy it, but more often I see it as something I have to do. In this, I am no different from many successful businesspeople who shut out distractions in order to do their work. I see them on the baseball fields with their Black-Berries and cell phones. Unfortunately, some of those distractions are soccer matches, weekends, family dinners. But in the pursuit of fame, fortune, or fill-in-the-blank, they do not allow themselves to get sidetracked by things they do not value. Like me, they do not let a simple thing like bad weather or a sore hamstring get in the way of their run.

Three miles, four miles, five miles. The February air feels bracing against my face, refreshing in my lungs. I think I can smell spring in the air, and perhaps I can. It is less than four weeks away, and with it the promise of renewal, growth, and rebirth. I stopped running every day when we moved to the suburbs, but now I think if I can find an hour to run at ten P.M. after flying six hours from the West Coast, I can certainly find an hour for dinner.

I return home, if not entirely a new man, a reinvigorated man, with a plan.

"How was the run?" Christine asks. She is unpacking the kids' clothes, tossing them into the laundry. Although it's late, we are on West Coast time, and sleep is several hours away. (Simon and Lulu, on the other hand, have crashed.)

"Beautiful," I say. I kiss her, and she pushes me away gently. "You're sweaty," she says.

"And I stink," I add.

"That, too."

I laugh and kiss her again, and this time she doesn't resist. Marriage, too, is a lot like running: There are good days and bad, and sometimes it seems as if the struggle isn't worth it, but just when you think you can't go on, there's a new day, a clear path, and a burst down the straightaway.

I have not always been the best husband, I know, or the easiest person to live with. There are days, I'm sure, when Christine would like to walk away from me—or strangle me. Over the years, I have grown more ornery and impatient, until I resemble a cranky widower in a recliner with a bourbon. But my intentions have always been good, even if my actions are less than perfect. This year has had its setbacks, and yet Christine has not asked for our old life back, even if she finds my constant/inconstant presence in the house unnerving at times. When awards are given for Most Likely to Thrive in Adverse Soil Conditions, she will win the blue ribbon.

"Come upstairs?" I ask.

And she does.

This is another truth about marriage: Sometimes the most familiar things are the most exciting, and the most exciting is the most familiar. My wife before the mirror, her hair to her shoulders, in a tank top, the cord of muscle twining up her neck.

The next morning we are awakened by Lulu, who bounces onto our bed like a beach ball. "Daddy," she says. "I'm hungry."

Her little face couldn't be more perfect, high-browed and quizzical, kissed a golden brown by the Los Angeles sun.

I rise up on my elbows. "What would you like to eat?"

"I don't know," she says. "What do we have?"

"Let's check."

I carry her downstairs and set her on the countertop while I make coffee. Sugar licks the tips of her toes as they dangle toward the floor. "Sugar!" Lulu complains.

"She wants breakfast, too," I say.

We feed Sugar, then Lulu. The two girls sit munching from a bowl, although not the same one.

While they eat, I pull a couple of cookbooks from the shelf. It's only eight o'clock, but I am already thinking about dinner. Now I understand why my own mother would ask me what I wanted for dinner first thing in the morning. Though I always found it annoying, there's a logic to planning the day that begins with the end. Meals require preparation, which requires a menu and a trip to the supermarket. These are not tasks for the organizationally challenged or easily intimidated. A little randomness is a good thing; too much, and you're microwaving chicken nuggets at six P.M.

Lulu reads over my shoulder as I review *Kid Food: Rachael Ray's Top 30 30-Minute Meals*. "Ziti!" she says, stopping me on a brightly photographed page of reds, whites, and yellows. I didn't know Lulu liked ziti, or even knew what it was, but she explains she has eaten it for lunch at school. Will wonders never cease?

Ziti, of course, is a natural for kids. The kind of thing they have been serving for school lunches since the Jurassic era. Pasta and cheese are two of the major food groups (chocolate milk is the third). But my kids are no ordinary eaters. Although my daughter will eat pasta and cheese, I have never seen her eat them together. When I offer to sprinkle Parmesan cheese over her plain pasta, for example, she squawks as if I've suggested I pull off her toenails. And while Simon also loves pasta in its myriad forms, he will hardly touch it with tomato sauce. So ziti is a risk.

But Lulu insists that's what she wants for dinner, and what Lulu wants . . . well, let's just say I'm a sucker for moon-faced, almond-eyed, fierce little girls who take no prisoners and don't let their brothers beat up on them—at least not without exacting a serious toll.

After breakfast I take Lulu with me to the supermarket. This is something we both enjoy, because she gets to pull coupons from the dispensers that line the aisles, and I get to take my time perusing the goods. Although the vastness of Stop & Shop can annoy me, particularly when I'm in a hurry (and its deliberate placement of dairy and vegetables at opposite ends of the store, forcing shoppers to traverse the no-man's-land of shampoos, pet foods, and "seasonal specials," makes me feel like a rat caught in a maze), today I wander, in no particular hurry, and neither is Lulu. The abundance of choices feels luxurious rather than conspicuous. Do

I want barbecued potato chips, sea salt and vinegar, jalapeño and cheese, "robust russet," or sour cream and dill? Lay's, Wise, Cape Cod, Utz, or Pringles? Family pack, travel, or "fun" sized? Maybe I don't want potato chips at all. Instead, I could buy "restaurant style" tortilla chips. But wait—with salt or without? Reduced fat or baked? Curled into perfect dipping size or the more familiar triangular shape? A man could get lost in the packaging alone.*

Lulu pulls down several packages of her favorite brand of potato chips, and I toss in the full-fat, fully salted tortilla chips. Live a little, I tell myself. Tomorrow we diet.

When we pass the books and video aisle, Lulu asks if she can buy a comic book. Of course she can, I say. She wants to know if she can get one for Simon, too. This is another difference between my children that I've observed this year: Lulu will often think about what Simon wants, but Simon rarely considers what Lulu would like. Maybe it's a gender thing, or a birth order difference, or just something that's hardwired into their genes like a predilection for salty snacks and Sour Patch candy. Whatever the reason, it strikes me that this a difference I would never have noticed last year. I saw the obvious: One is a boy, the other a girl; one has blond hair, the other has brown. But their subtle tastes and preferences (Simon dislikes chocolate and prefers the yellow LifeSavers; Lulu favors Pez, sourballs, and jawbreakers) escaped me.

We buy the food and two comic books. I resist Lulu's entreaties to purchase bubble gum. It's still early enough to have breakfast, and Lulu tends to stick the gum on my car seat (another astute observation I've made this year).

Spring break is over tomorrow, so we spend the rest of the day

---

* Americans ate 6.5 billion pounds of salty snack foods last year, a market that is worth $21 billion, according to Mintel International Group.

retrieving and cleaning out backpacks, organizing papers, making another trip to the supermarket for the lunch items I forgot, finding the ice packs for the lunch boxes, and putting away the clothes Christine has washed and the ones the kids threw all over their room in their packing haste before we left. It's warm enough to go outside, and in the afternoon Simon and I play basketball on the driveway, then MLB baseball on the PlayStation. I win the basketball game, but he slaughters me on the PlayStation, hitting a grand slam in the bottom of the ninth and sending the Red Sox to another ignominious defeat at the hands of the dreaded Yankees.

I decline a rematch to go for a run. My legs are beat up from the night before, but I've never let a little lactic acid stop me. Although the first mile is painful, my muscles relax with the influx of blood, and soon I am cruising home. After the run, it's time to make dinner. Lulu helps prepare the roux by whisking flour into a small bowl of milk. I boil the pasta until it's about two minutes short of al dente. We make a simple tomato sauce with a can of crushed tomatoes, some garlic, onion powder (no real onions for Lulu), and oregano. After laying the pasta in a casserole dish, Lulu has fun pouring the milk, then the tomato sauce and cheese over the top.

When the ziti emerges from the oven, steaming and bubbling with cheese, I know I've got a hit. Lulu is excited to sample a meal she tells Simon she prepared, and Simon says Lulu's ziti is better than the stuff from the cafeteria. I learn another lesson: The more hands that make the meal, the more mouths it will feed. We finish most of the casserole dish and retire peacefully, happily, and sated.

Drawn back into work, I find the week passes quickly. By Thursday, I have already missed two dinners at home. That night I am invited out for drinks by a colleague. In a former life I would have accepted the invitation, stayed late, had a drink, come home after my kids were asleep, and missed another opportunity to see them. Instead, I keep tabs on every meal, every time I am at home, and every time I miss dinner. I used to keep a training log, with each workout neatly noted: *12 × 400m, 66–68 seconds, 90 seconds recovery.* If I missed a day, I would mark the page with a big red *X,* a sign of disappointment and a reminder to try harder next time. Now I keep a web log, where I note every success and every failure and measure my progress by dinners. Five nights a week. Ten nights in a row. I decline the invitation.

Parents need rules, I decide, just as kids do. It's too easy to let the important things slip away, lose track of time, forget that children are young for an extremely short window before they move away, fall in love, raise their own families. Even in the happiest scenario—where best intentions and extracurricular activities cooperate—I will never be able to have dinner with them five nights a week for more than another handful of years. Do I really want to trade that time for a drink with a person whose name I will probably forget within the decade?

I rush home and get there just in time to sit down to penne with pesto. We play a round of "Is it true?" and then I help Simon with his math homework while Lulu practices piano with Christine. I have begun to get the hang of this new, improved mathematics, in which a rhombus is likely to make a surprise appearance at a party of parallelograms. Later, we trade children, and I read Lulu our favorite bedtime story, *The Story of Ferdinand,* in my best Spanish accent while Christine and Simon review his spelling words. When the kids are asleep, I clean the kitchen and Christine finishes some freelance editing work. Then the adults go upstairs, get into bed, and share magazines until lights-out.

On Friday, I work in my Westport office. I have three nights left to make one and a half meals, so I'm already scouting recipes. For Friday, I decide I will make orzo with saffron, an easy dish that requires just butter, Parmesan cheese, and saffron, ideal for the father who's rushing home at 5:05. It's a simple variation on a dish that Lulu eats all the time: pasta with butter. Except it has a little yellow coloring, some cheese, and a subtle flowery taste from the most expensive spice in the world. Nevertheless, despite our recent experience with ziti, Lulu will not eat it, although Simon does. Instead of getting angry, I tell myself that a 75 percent approval rating would make any politician happy. I'm not a politician, exactly, but I'm beginning to understand about getting to yes. On the roads, winning is about more than crossing the finish line in first place. There are personal records, and private demons, and small triumphs. Sometimes finishing is the achievement itself.

Christine makes popcorn, we sit down to watch a movie, and both kids tuck in next to me on the couch. Lulu falls asleep before the movie ends, and I carry her upstairs, her head nestled against my shoulder, legs draped over my arm. I kiss her lightly on the forehead, then pull the covers around her. She makes a noise as if she's kissing me back, her lips pursing and relaxing repeatedly, and I realize she's having a dream of nursing. It was not that long ago that Christine lay with Lulu in this same bed, engaged in one of the most basic mammalian activities. Though I often measure time by distance, sometimes, I think, things are closer than they appear. Yes, my children are growing fast, tall, straight, but they are still children, in need of care and feeding and the occasional stiff drink of apple juice. And I am just the dad for the job.

We finish our movie, and Christine puts Simon to bed while I straighten a family room that looks as if popcorn has rained down from the heavens. Sugar helps, but there are too many kernels stuck between the pillows on the couch for her to be of much use. Instead, she licks the salt from my fingers, her tongue smacking like a licorice whip. I take her outside for a last, quick walk, and she does her business in a favorite spot. By the time I get upstairs, the lights are out and everyone is asleep. Even the house is sighing.

I manage to run both weekend days, ignoring sore hamstrings and recurrent Achilles tendinitis. On Sunday, I stretch the run to nearly nine miles, a long loop that takes me past horse farms into a glimpse of Fairfield County before it was overrun with McMansions and shopping plazas. The smell of decaying leaves fills the air, an acrid-sweet scent not unlike that of an unlit cigar. I turn down Hulls Farm Road and feel the wind at my back, gently pushing me forward. The sky is clear, the sun is bright, and for a moment I feel as if I am twenty-eight again, my muscles singing, the open road beckoning. I pick up my pace, and soon I am flying along the pavement: arms pumping, legs churning, lungs gulping, itching to get home.

I'm hungry; there's pasta cooking; and I have miles to go before I eat.

Mealtime with Mom

Take one hungry man. Add beer, pretzels, four cups coffee. Mix, shake, and serve. The resulting concoction is sure to turn everyone's stomach.

By the time I arrive home from New York, I am in a foul mood. It's been one of those days when the line of students through my office never relented, the phone rang and rang, and my editor loved the piece I wrote and wanted to know when I could rewrite the entire thing ("How about Wednesday?" she asked. "How about never?" I countered). The good news is that I have begun to get my own clients; the bad news is that I have begun to get my own clients. The lull in work is over, and with it fears of bankruptcy. Although I have not returned to my pre–Dinner with Dad income, I have not had to dip into our home equity line of credit this month. This should make me happy; instead, it just makes me tired. Or maybe it's the Foster's lager I consumed on the train.

Everything changes when I walk in the door.

"Daddy!" calls Lulu, as if I've just returned from a battlefield. She runs to me, arms extended, and I lift her in the air, exactly as Jimmy Stewart might do, except this isn't a big screen; it's my small kitchen, my own house, my own daughter. Sugar quickly follows her, and licks my shins as if I am a lollipop.

"Hello, girls," I say. "What's happening?"

"We had a fiesta today, and I broke the piñata," says Lulu. She displays a fistful of candy triumphantly.

Simon looks up from the kitchen table, where he has been reading a guide to the mysteries of Harry Potter. "Lulu said I could have the yellow Starburst."

"I did," says Lulu, generous as always.

There's something different in the house, and it's not just the contrast between the gloom of the commuter train and the effervescence of my children.

Then I notice it: the smell of frying hamburgers.

"Christine?" I venture.

She stands in front of the stove, spatula in hand, carefully scrutinizing the cast-iron skillet as if it might contain something radioactive. "Oh! You scared me!" she says when I give her a quick kiss on the neck. Then, following my gaze, she says, "I thought we might have hamburgers," as if it were the most normal thing in the world.

Yes, Christine has overcome her strict aversion to the flesh of animals—at least enough to serve chicken and hot dogs to her children. She has even served me steak on the rare occasion (no pun intended). But I never thought I'd see the day when she would fry up four burgers for the entire family.

"They smell good, don't they?"

I agree; there's nothing beats the smell of a grilled hamburger.

"Are you having one, too?"

She shakes her head. Although hamburgers were the last animal product she gave up, and even though she's tempted by the smell, she can't bring herself to eat one.

So what explains this change of heart, this deviation from the vegetarian credo?

"I guess I thought it was unfair that I was keeping you from eating something you liked."

"Really?" I ask, as if Christine could be capable of subterfuge.

"Really," she repeats. "You've been trying all these new foods, so I thought I would, too."

Miracles will never cease. Or maybe it's my dessert for all the good food I've put on her plate this year.

"Something like that," she says with a grin. "Now get out of here. You're making me nervous."

I retreat to the kitchen table with the kids, challenging them to a thumb wrestle while we wait for dinner to be served. Lulu wins four matches and Simon wins five before Christine arrives with the plate of meat. She deals out patties like a short-order cook, slipping them onto our plates with a flourish of the wrist.

"Mom, do you have ketchup?" asks Lulu, who has come to think of ketchup as the indispensable condiment, second only to salt.

Christine gives Lulu a squirt, then sits at the head of the table, where Sugar awaits her patiently as if expecting a cheeseburger. "You already had dinner," she says to the dog. If Sugar understands, she doesn't let on; instead, she thumps her tail against the floor, hoping for a break. Christine ignores her and unwraps her microwaved vegetarian burrito.

"That's so sad," I say, indicating the burrito.

"Don't get cocky," she replies.

We dig into our burgers. They are tasty and delicious, the thick taste of meat nothing like the watery taste of tofu.

"Is it cooked enough?" asks Christine, for whom the slightest sight of pink conjures all kinds of gruesome images.

"It's perfect," I say.

"More ketchup," says Lulu, indicating her plate, before popping the rest of one burger into her mouth. She eats both without the buns, which may be more food than she's ever consumed in a single sitting. I have mine with avocados and tomatoes. Simon has one, and passes on the second ("I like hot dogs better," he concludes). There are onion rings and a generous salad, and the whole affair feels like a barbecue on the beach, even though it's forty degrees outside.

"How do you feel?" I ask Christine, because I know feeding meat to her children makes her uneasy. The first time Simon came home from a party and told us he ate a hot dog, her face literally blanched, and it was all I could do to stop her from calling up the boy's mother and letting loose.

"I feel okay," she says. "I'm happy to see Lulu eat so much. It makes me feel like maybe I should have been giving her hamburgers all along."

I understand Christine's feelings. I have felt the same way for much of this year. There's a powerful emotion when your children eat your food that is about more than just feeding someone. It's a deep primordial feeling, born in the primitive brain. The sense of fulfilling your role as provider, of nourishing your own kin, of feeding the future. It's the reason why having children reject your food feels so painful, more than it would if they were just houseguests (or someone else's children) who didn't like the sauce you made for the pasta. A cook doesn't have to take it personally,* but a parent literally lives to feed the next generation.

* Of course sometimes the best chefs *do* take it personally, not because they think of their customers as their children, but because they think of the food as their baby.

So what's a little hamburger compared to survival?

Of course, it's easy to lose the connection between food and life. When you start reheating chicken nuggets or microwaving meals to go, when you give in to the demands for Coca-Cola and Big Macs, when dinner becomes about refueling rather than nourishing, a parent can disconnect from his role in the process. No one feels bad when her child refuses to finish her Big Mac (as rare as that might be). It's industrial food, without a personal connection, which might explain, in part, why parents choose fast food (besides the convenience): to avoid the messy emotional entanglements.

But now Christine has joined me on the long road back, each of us disconnected in our own way, each of us making an attempt to reclaim the personal. For me it has come in the form of *being there* for dinner, in both an existential and a literal sense. For Christine, who has always been there, it's about rediscovering her power to feed her children rather than simply checking the box next to caloric intake. If it means relinquishing some of her beliefs, at least the beef will be grass fed and organic, free of antibiotics and pesticides, and humanely raised and slaughtered.

After dinner, Simon clears the table without protest, and I rinse the dishes and place them in the dishwasher. We clean the counters together, and when all is straightened up, we retire to my office to review Simon's homework. Simon's work habits remind me of my own: his goal is speed, not accuracy. As a boy, I raced to finish books, jump ahead to the next reading group, put my pencil down first. In law school, I rarely took notes, and lacked the discipline to create the prodigious outlines undertaken by some of my classmates. Even now, I find myself skimming material I should read thoroughly, or relying on memory when I should refer to the text. Watching my own son repeat some of my bad habits makes me want to correct him for both our benefits. Yet I have learned enough this year to know I should hold my tongue. No amount of scolding will change his proclivities—just as yelling at my daughter to eat artichokes will not turn her into a gourmand. Better to demonstrate by doing, to teach by calm modeling, rather than ranting.

This is the reason we have parents: to mend the error of our ways, and steer us in the right direction. Or at least to buy the Band-Aids. But a steer is not a push, and I am careful when I suggest to Simon he might want to reread a question. He does, notices his mistake, and crosses out his previous answer in bold pen strokes, leaving his paper a bluish mess. Although it's not exactly what I intended, I take it as a favorable sign, and we move quickly through the remaining problems.

Then it's upstairs, into pajamas, teeth brushed, shades drawn, book read, lights out. An evening, a nighttime, another day.

Parenting is a team effort. It's easy to forget this as you're trudging to the station at six in the morning and eating your dinner coming home on the train. In those circumstances, parenting can seem like a one-way street, all the traffic flowing in one direction. Why come home at all? Why not just write a check, see the kids on the weekend, sleep in a studio apartment? It's hard to feel like part of a team when you're running alone.

Although I had not quite reached the depths of despondency, making dinner with my family has made me appreciate Christine's efforts to keep our children healthy and to introduce good food into their diets, as well as the enormity of the task. Absence does not make the heart grow fonder; to the contrary, it hardens the heart, makes it shrivel and crack, until there is nothing left but a small, efficient pump, good for only a few ragged beats.

This is what I think, anyway, as I come home to a flurry of home-cooked meals. Broiled tilapia. Fresh lemon sole. Barbecued chicken with spinach and shredded carrots. Though Christine doesn't have much more luck than I getting our children to eat more than a bite of fish, the food is good and varied, and arrives on the plate with green side dishes and carbohydrates like a meal from the pages of a glossy magazine. It's dinner the way it ought to be, the way it is often imagined but rarely achieved, and it would be perfect if not for the cries of the children at the table who think fish and spinach are the edible equivalents of toxic waste.

"Fish is brain food," I say.

"Gross," says Lulu.

I laugh, partly because it's not my meal being criticized, but also because it's hard to take a scowling six-year-old seriously, especially when everyone is sitting around the same table, my son is trying his best not to spit out his food, the dog is waiting anxiously for him to do so, my wife is flushed from the heat of the oven, and I can feel the tugs of a family bond tightening around us, drawing us closer together in a way we haven't been for several years.

It's not just Dinner with Dad. It's dinner with Mom, and Simon, and Lulu, and Sugar. Cooking together has restored some of the equilibrium to our life, a balance lost when I worked all the time, Christine cooked all the time, and the kids were worse for the trade-off. I don't know if our new arrangements will protect us from substance abuse, obesity, and illegal file sharing, but it sure feels good—and tastes even better.

That's on Friday. The following Monday I return on the 5:23 to what can charitably be described as "chickpea surprise." This is a dish that features both chickpeas and spaghetti, as if there weren't enough carbohydrates in one to compensate for the other. The "sauce" appears to be comprised of feta cheese and garlic, a potent combination, certain to ward off evil spirits and all but the bravest (or most foolish) eaters. I've never been a big fan of feta cheese—too crumbly, creamy, cheesy—and this meal isn't going to change my mind any time soon.

For the kids, Christine hasn't even bothered to win converts. She serves them pasta with butter. One difference between us is that Christine begins a meal by assuming the kids won't eat it and plans accordingly, while I assume they will. This either makes her a realist or me naïve, or both.

"Is there enough pasta for me?" I ask.

Another difference is that Christine can laugh about her failures, while I would sulk. Unlike her popovers, which were perfect, this dish is practically inedible.

"It's not as if everything you've made has been delicious," she says, the slightest bit defensive.

"What didn't you like?" I ask.

"Baked stuffed potatoes? White chili? Raclette?"

I nod soberly. She's right. In a year of new achievements, there are bound to be some debacles. You can't make an omelet without breaking a few eggs—or spoiling them. The slippery scrod is gone, but not entirely forgotten.

We toss the spaghetti/chickpea combo into the garbage, although not without a certain reluctance. This meal could feed plenty of hungry people, who might appreciate the double dose of carbohydrates. The dark side of picky eating is the sheer waste of food, the meats and vegetables we toss every day, the pasta with the unappealing sauce, the rice that has sat in the refrigerator for one day too many, neglected but not inedible. My own parents would threaten to mail the meals to "starving children in Africa," which always struck me as a punishment for them, not for me. Still, I find myself lecturing my children about Darfur and Rwanda, even as I scrape the food into the trash.

"Dad—you eat it," Simon finally says, which stops me in my tracks. Talk about calling a bluff. There's string, and paper, and lots of stamps, but this food isn't being mailed anywhere.

We finish cleaning, then climb the stairs for the postgame interview. It's all Christine can do to stop from laughing, remembering the look on my face, the chickpeas no longer a bad dinner but a good joke. Lulu races into Simon's room and jumps on his bed, causing the slats underneath to slip from their brackets and sending the mattress to the floor with a thump. By the time Lulu is extricated, the dog is pacified, and Simon is appeased, dinner is a distant memory and it's time for dreaming.

"Are you going to put this on your blog?" Christine asks.

"No," I lie.

"You should," she says. "It's funny."

The funniest meal of the year, however, arrives on our plates several weeks later in the form of spaghetti carbonara that Christine has made from a recipe she finds in a fancy Italian cookbook. In keeping with her newfound discovery of animal flesh, Christine has scoured the aisles at Wild Oats for organic, free-range turkey bacon, which she spends the better part of a half-hour chopping and frying, washing her hands as thoroughly as Lady Macbeth when she's finished. But despite these admirable and hygienic efforts, the spaghetti is accompanied by a watery sauce that purports to be comprised of eggs and cream. Lulu takes one look at it and howls her disapproval. Simon is calmer, but he, too, regards the meal as a petri dish for bacterial infections. This time, Christine is not amused.

"You better take a bite," she warns the children. "That bacon cost me eight dollars."

"Christine," I say. "These eggs are raw."

"They are not raw," she insists. "I followed the recipe."

I push the spaghetti around my plate, but it's clear to me that something has gone terribly wrong here. Of course, there's nothing necessarily wrong with raw eggs—they are one of the ingredients in Caesar salad dressing and mayonnaise, among other things. But something about the combination of raw eggs and turkey bacon is a recipe for disaster—or salmonella.

"I spent a lot of time cooking this," says Christine.

"I'll try it," I say, making a silent plea to the gods of antimicrobial stomach acids. I twirl several strands around my fork, chew lightly, and swallow. Christine looks at me expectantly, and I don't frown at her so much as ask for a reprieve.

"Have another bite," she says.

This is my wife, I tell myself, and she is only looking out for my interests—as well as those of our children, and our dog. She has been my witting partner in this adventure for eight months, and while many others might have given up the first time I lost my temper, she has taken it in stride, understanding that Dinner with Dad is about more than just food, or cooking, or even good taste. No matter how the year ends—at the table, in a restaurant, or on a hospital gurney—she will still be there beside me, urging me onward, tempting me to take another bite, forgiving me the error of my ways.

I take another bite. It does not taste any better.

Eventually, Christine is convinced the food needs to be returned to the stove. Perhaps in the perfect world of fancy Italian food writers, raw eggs will combine with hot spaghetti and bacon in a perfect alchemy. But at our dinner table, we like our food cooked. Even the vegetarians.

"I tried," Christine says later, teeth resting on her bottom lip like tombstones.

I take her in my arms and give her a kiss. "It was fine," I say. "After you cooked it."

"I wanted to make something special."

"You did." I tick off her successes: tilapia, salmon, sole, chili, tofu, couscous, chickpeas (without spaghetti), lasagna, and fresh pesto, to say nothing of hamburgers and hot dogs and some amazing salads, cookies, and cakes. In a year of Dinner with Dad, Mealtime with Mom has been a significant corollary benefit. Since

September, our dinners have owed their bountiful variety to a two-person operation. Each has his (or her) weaknesses but each his strengths, as well. For every failed attempt at something new, there have been multiple successes at the odd, unheralded, unknown, and untried. The secret, it seems to me, is to keep going—keep mixing, stirring, chopping, dicing, kneading, salting, tasting, cooking. Today's undercooked spaghetti carbonara is tomorrow's excellent fettuccine Alfredo.

"Do you think I should have used real bacon?" Christine asks.

I remember the days of real bacon as if they were yesterday instead of fifteen years ago. Back then, we didn't worry about cholesterol, pig products, mortgage payments. "I miss bacon," I say.

"I used to love bacon," says Christine.

"And pork sausages."

"Pork chops."

"Pork rinds."

"Pork bellies."

And we're off. A new day. A new meal. A forgotten delight, now remembered.

TV Dinner

My thumbs hurt.

I am tapping out a text message to my brother on my cell phone when I realize the steady throbbing in my joints is actually the result of too much time spent talking—with my hands. I have recently discovered how to send a text message, and now I'm overusing it like a teenager at a disco, or like my own students who appear to be taking furious notes but are actually IMing someone they just met on MySpace. *R u coming up 2morrow?* I write in the strange half-language of electronic communication. *Call u l8r,* he promises.

When I gave up my job in Kansas City I was stripped of my BlackBerry like an officer demoted in rank. I went from being a captain of industry to a lowly private with a cell phone (without camera!) and Palm. I gazed at my fellow commuters with envy as they caught up on e-mail before arriving at the office and pretended to be working late as they made the early train

202 ••• Cameron Stracher

home.* Mostly, though, I just missed the feeling of having a shiny toy that magically sent words through the ether and buzzed me lovingly on the hip when new words arrived.

The truth is I love technology with all its pitfalls and promises. This explains why I bought computers for my children as soon as they could read, installed iTunes, gave my son a Nano and my wife an iPod shuffle, and encouraged the birthday purchases of a PlayStation and Nintendo DS. But like a gadget junkie, I cannot shut my habit off. I realize this when I come home from my Westport office and run to check my e-mail only five minutes after checking it last. It's not as if anything could happen in the short drive back to my house, or that I'm not instantly reachable on my cell phone anyway. Rather, I crave the soothing narcotic of Outlook Express, the overflowing in-box, the constant contact with the digital world. It's time to face facts: My name is Cam, and I'm an e-mail addict.

This is a problem. In my struggle to spend more time with my family, my e-mail addiction is a black hole into which the minutes disappear. Not only does it physically remove me, it removes me emotionally as well. When my daughter comes into my office and asks me a question, I respond to her in the half-drugged voice of someone who is multitasking and unable to focus on what she wants. After she leaves, I hear her calling for her mother to ask the same question. I almost rise from my chair to go after her, but three more messages arrive that demand immediate responses.

But like father, like son—and daughter. When I walk upstairs to call the kids down for dinner, Simon is on the PlayStation and

---

* Although BlackBerry installs a helpful "Sent from my BlackBerry Wireless Handheld" tag on the bottom of every e-mail, the savvy commuter knows how to disable the message because it's the equivalent of broadcasting, "Went home early today."

Lulu is playing a game on her computer. It takes several attempts to draw them away, and Simon has that glazed look in his eyes common to video and morphine addicts. He is surly, too, answering his mother's questions as if he were a truculent sixteen-year-old instead of two weeks short of his tenth birthday. Though his PlayStation games are "age appropriate," they include car chases where the goal is to evade the police, and baseball games where the goal is to knock down the first baseman and catcher. Is it any wonder his attitude is best described as aggressively indifferent?

When I add up all my children's screen time for the day—computers, PlayStation, Nintendo, TV—I am shocked to discover it comes to nearly three hours each.* This is time that simply didn't exist when we were children. Instead of MLB 2006, my friends and I played Strat-O-Matic baseball, a board game that at least required interaction with other people and didn't overstimulate us with rapidly changing colors and images. There were no cartoons during the week, and on the weekends none of the children in *The Jetsons* called their parents "buttheads." We couldn't communicate except through face-to-face contact, and even once we had telephone privileges the only places we could talk were easily monitored by adults. Of course, we also had to walk five miles through the snow in our bare feet just to get to school, but that was only when the horse was lame.

We eat a quick meal, and the children race from the table as soon as they are finished. Though Christine calls out after them

---

* Thirty minutes of TV watching before school; one hour after school; forty-five minutes of PlayStation/Nintendo while dinner is being prepared; thirty minutes of computer/e-mail/Internet before bed. In this, however, they are below average. According to the American Academy of Pediatrics, the typical child spends four hours a day watching TV and will see more than twenty thousand commercials in a year. He also plays about seven hours of video games a week, according to the National Institute on Media and the Family.

"No TV!" they have soon escaped into the world behind an LCD screen. Meanwhile, instead of finishing the book I have been reading for three weeks, I retreat to my e-mail, answering the five messages that arrived in the last half-hour and sending a dozen new ones. Christine is in her own office, shopping for vintage Archie comics for Simon on eBay. It is nearly 8:30 P.M. before we both emerge to put the children to bed.

"Five more minutes!" Simon protests. "It's the fourth quarter!"

It's always the fourth quarter, or the ninth inning, or seven seconds left on the shot clock. But when I give him five more minutes, I return to find him immersed in another game.

"Simon!" I scold, taking the controller out of his hands.

He allows himself to be dragged from the television, one eye on the screen as we make our way to the bathroom. When we are finally out of view, he tells me he has a math assignment due in the morning.

"I thought you already did your homework," I say.

"That was regular homework. This is enrichment."

By now it is 9:15 P.M., too late to sit down to do mathematics. But trying to get Simon to do anything in the morning is like threading a needle with a bicycle chain. So we grab a few pencils and some paper and clear a space on his desk amid the clutter of baseball cards, computer games, and comic books.

If Dad can make dinner in 30 minutes, and his children can eat it in 5, how much time does the family spend together in an evening?

The answer is that dinner may be a necessary, but it is not a sufficient condition of slenderness, math prowess, better SAT scores. Families who eat together may spend less time watching television, but there's still no guarantee everyone won't rush off to his screen after gobbling his meal. Togetherness can't be e-mailed as an attachment to our children's in-box, but must be built one bite at a time.

We finish the homework and I kiss Simon goodnight, then cross the hall to kiss Lulu but she's already asleep. Although I've been home for nearly four hours, I realize I've spent about seven minutes with Lulu tonight, and if not for his math homework, I would have spent the same amount of time with Simon.

"The kids watch too much television," I say to Christine as we are preparing for bed, as if it were their fault and not mine.

"I know," she says. "Today was a bad day."

"I should have read Lulu a book," I say mournfully.

"She's okay."

Though I know my daughter will survive one night without Ferdinand, I wonder if I am winning the battle but losing the war. Coming home on time serves no purpose if I treat my home like an office and my children like coworkers. It's a conflict I didn't have at the beginning of the year, but a conflict nonetheless, not ameliorated by my apparent helplessness against electronic demons.

The next day, feeling guilty, I make one of Lulu's favorites: fresh pasta. I buy a pasta machine, which makes cutting the dough a cinch. Lulu cranks the handle while I feed the dough, and the perfect strands of linguine-sized pasta that emerge look like Play-Doh. While I simmer a tomato sauce, Lulu invites a friend for dinner and a sleepover. I hear her saying, "You're really going to like my dad's pasta!" When the friend arrives they run upstairs, but they come back downstairs for dinner with a bounce (and without a second summons). They slurp the curly noodles quickly, leaving butter on their chins, then run back off to play. Simon, Christine, and I have a second helping, and suddenly I don't feel neglectful or inattentive. A satisfied customer is a dad's best medicine, warding off demons with more potency than garlic.

Simon clears the table, and Christine and I rinse the plates and load the dishwasher. Simon wants to watch the Yankees game with me, so Christine makes popcorn for both of us, then takes another bowl upstairs to the girls. Though we are divided along gender lines, *and* watching television, it feels different from when we are each in our electronic isolation. I love snuggling with Simon on the couch, dropping popcorn in our laps, and watching Derek Jeter beat out an infield single. The problem with electronics, I realize, is the plethora of choices: PlayStation for Simon, Nintendo for Lulu, e-mail for me, Internet for Christine. It is another example of a culture that has successfully marketed to the individual, creating a demand for four televisions instead of one, five telephone lines instead of two, a computer in every room, a handheld in every palm, a foil-wrapped meal for one. What we think of as our individuality is really just our isolation. Though the BlackBerry makes it possible to sneak out of work early, it also encourages private communication to colleagues from the sidelines of your daughter's soccer game—a familiar sight on the Westport fields.

If Dad spends 45 minutes watching his daughter play soccer while text-messaging his brother, how many plays has he seen?

Sometimes we must have our freedom wrenched from our hands like an enemy's flag. Though most of us could not live without our devices, the fact is we did, and we could. I am not a Luddite, and I will give up my iPod when it is pried from my cold, dead fingers, but sitting with Simon on the couch I realize I need to find the "off" switch on my computer.* Otherwise, dinner will be a Pyrrhic victory, my efforts beaten by the very devices intended to set me free.

---

* In fact, there is no "off" button on a Windows computer; turning off the computer requires clicking on the "Start" tab, which used to strike me as a design flaw but now seems ingenious because it calls up lots of other options that encourage keeping the computer on.

In that spirit, I vow not to check my e-mail for the entire weekend. This is easier said than done—twice I find myself literally itching to click on the Outlook icon, and I am saved only because once Lulu catches me in the act and the other time my automatic backup software causes the machine to crash. On Sunday afternoon, however, my cell phone rings, a client calling to inform me of a potential lawsuit. Simon and I are playing basketball on the driveway, and I have to walk away, stand in the middle of our front yard, and discuss the invasion-of-privacy tort for fifteen minutes. By the time I return, Simon is inside the house watching television.

"Come back outside," I say.

"It's boring," he says.

"You're scared, because I was thrashing you."

That does it. He jumps from the couch, and we play until Christine calls us for dinner.

"Last shot, Dad," says Simon. I take it and miss, and Simon rebounds the ball, then drives past me for the layup.

"No fair," I say.

He touches his chest twice with his fist, kisses his hand, then points one finger toward the sky, a perfect mimic of players he's seen on television. I kick at his shins with my toe, and we both laugh, enjoying the idea of the five-foot son outplaying his six-foot father. Simon bounces the ball into the garage, and we head inside for dinner.

At the table, Christine announces a new family rule: one hour of screen time per day. This sparks a debate and some lawyerlike discussion: Can Simon play Nintendo *while* watching a Yankee game, or does this count as double time? (Christine says it's two activities.) Does loading music from a computer onto a Nano count as screen time? (Yes, says Christine.) Is Dad exempt from the rule? (Yes, but only if he really has to work.) There's surprisingly little protest, perhaps because our children still don't really have a precise grasp of time—an hour can seem like a day, a minute like an hour—and they have fun that first night stopping the clock after twenty-three minutes on the computer and asking how much time they have left.

The screen limit helps me as well, because during the thirty-seven minutes that Lulu plays Nintendogs, I can check my e-mail with impunity. But when her buzzer goes off, that's the signal for me to stop, too. There's a minor disagreement when Simon's time runs out just as Robinson Cano is batting with two on and two out, and both he and I want to see the result, but Christine reminds me it's a slippery slope from five more minutes to the rest of the game, and there are 162 games to negotiate every year. She needs to say no more.

By the time the following weekend rolls around, we are immersed in our new schedule, the deprivation from our beloved devices scarcely noticed. Lulu is playing softball and Simon is playing baseball, and I have somehow agreed to coach both teams, which means I dash from field to field with four heavy bags of equipment, bats and balls of various sizes, and enough water to stock a cross-country trip. Because I planned on watching the games anyway, I reasoned coaching would not require much more time, but I've underestimated how long it takes to figure out batting lineups and field positions, and the extra days devoted to practice. When Simon's game is over, I feel as if I have run a marathon and babysat twenty-four children, which is not that far from the truth.

Nevertheless, I go for a real run when we get home, a five-mile jaunt along the narrow roads, my feet aching from standing for several hours, my back stiff and neck sore. If forty-five is the new thirty, no one has told my muscles. I try to stay on the grass that borders the roads, sidewalks being too urban for our quaint New England town. I jog past gardeners at work, blowing sticks and leaves into neat piles for disposal, and step over crocuses pushing up through their beds. At a stop sign, a car honks at me, and two boys—Simon's teammates—wave as they drive past. Unconsciously, I lengthen my stride, lifting my knees and gathering momentum.

They say for every year of a love affair, it takes half as long to recover. We lived in New York City for nine years, and have lived in the suburbs for four and a half, and for the first time when I think about leaving New York I don't feel as if my heart is broken. For all its flaws, expensive housing, SUV-infested roads, lengthy commute, Westport is my home, and I feel as if I belong. I'm not exactly sure when this happened—perhaps when I started recognizing people in the supermarket and the Starbucks, or maybe when the same kids I coached in the fall are on my team again in the spring—but I know that when I think of our small apartment in New York, it is not with a pang of longing, a stiff-upper-lippedness that comes from discarding your own dreams in favor of your children's. That time, long ago, has faded to a pleasant buzz rather than a nasty wound. It seems as far away as Alcatraz.

"I'm home," I announce, as I step into the kitchen.

If I expect some grand reception, I don't receive it. Instead, Sugar slobbers over my sweaty and salty calves until I push her away. "Where is everyone?" I ask. She doesn't answer.

I wander upstairs and eventually find both children sitting in Lulu's bed, listening to Christine read them a story. Sugar follows me in, and we both sit at Christine's feet. For all our technology, there's nothing like the human voice. Immediate, vibrant, stirring, and warm, it connects us in a way all the handhelds in the world cannot. Christine is a good reader, and we sit transfixed by her tale. When she's finished, Lulu wants to hear another, but we have guests coming for dinner and there's little time to prepare. Simon doesn't walk down the stairs so much as hurdle them, landing with an enormous thump on the first floor. Lulu laughs and races him to the kitchen, where they both wipe out against the baseboards, falling into a tangle on the tile. Sugar piles on, and soon they are twisted in one big knot: brother, sister, and dog, blond hair and golden fur, tail, legs, and teeth.

"Please," I say. "Don't break any bones."

"*Da*-ad," says Simon.

It's warm enough to wheel out the barbecue and blow off the dust. Our neighbors arrive with salad and dessert and three bottles of wine. Christine has bought salmon steaks, and for the kids there's pasta, butter, cheese, and hot dogs. We feed them first, then retire outside. A Chardonnay is uncorked and glasses poured, and soon we are sitting on the patio sipping our fermented grapes as the crickets emerge.

There's something to be said for the old way of doing business: feeding the kids, then concentrating on the adults. For one thing, the conversation is usually not interrupted with "Don't throw that!" or "Stop kicking your sister!" There's also no debate about who will try the spinach salad with goat cheese, walnuts, and mandarin orange slices. When the salmon is grilled, no one will pick at the crispy edges and claim it's burnt. And no one will call asparagus "aspara-piss."

But new technology has its place, especially after a dodgeball game breaks out in the family room. Sometimes a DVD player is the only thing that comes between a man and a tantrum. It's hard to believe that a laser-etched series of 1s and 0s can create such happiness or yield 100 minutes of peace and quiet, but I don't profess to understand the deeper workings of the universe, or the wonders of the silicon chip.

As I meander back outside with my third glass of wine, I am grateful for these things: good neighbors, good food, and good audio-video connections.

Knocking on Gnocchi's Door

Simon is a trouper.

"Are you coming home early or late?" he asks.

"Early," I promise.

He gives me a kiss and runs for the bus. For lunch he carries a turkey sandwich with cucumbers, which I know because I made it. While this might not sound unusual (I have personally consumed about 3,500 turkey sandwiches in my life), for Simon it's a breakthrough. After years of eating Goldfish, crackers, and grapes for lunch, then pizza, hot dogs, and chicken nuggets, he has agreed to pack a turkey sandwich. Suddenly, all his food objections have dissipated, scattered to the wind like cellophane. Although he still has his preferences, he is willing to try nearly anything once. Hamburger is a new favorite dish, as are falafel and risotto. The boy who could barely endure peanut butter is now wolfing down pad thai, chow fun, and edamame.

Lulu, on the other hand, remains an enigma wrapped in a riddle inside a conundrum. She has stopped eating my ziti, though she once purported to love it, claiming I no longer make it the same way (which is ridiculous). Fried chicken is hit or miss.* Even butter has become a no-no on her pasta.

One step forward, five steps back.

Perhaps all children must go through this phase, a right of passage that precedes tattoos but comes after toilet training. I've noticed that her friends tend to be as picky as she. The little girl who will only eat curly fries. The other friend who survives on mashed potatoes. It seems as if each child's picky eating habits are not quite the same, so that the parent who makes plain pasta for two girls must salt one dish and butter the other, place one in a bowl and the other on a plate. It's enough to drive a man insane.

To preserve my sanity, I have fallen back on the old standards: pesto pasta, pizza, grilled cheese sandwiches. If truth be told, I am in a slump, bored with my own choices, mired in comfort food and unable to summon the energy to overcome my daughter's insipid tastes. When I think of what to cook, I imagine resistance, and it's enough to make me avoid the unusual and unproven.

Today, though, I can hardly blame her. She sleeps on the couch, the victim of a stomach bug that makes the thought of eating anything nauseating.

"How is she?" I ask Christine.

"She had some toast. I told her she could watch *Powerpuff Girls*."

We both look at Lulu, silently thinking the same thought. A child's illness is a painful thing, worse than your own (I had this bug, and it's not pleasant). At that moment, she opens one eye and asks, "Can I have a juice bar?"

---

* She will, for example, eat chicken nuggets at the diner but not from Bell & Evans; and she refuses to touch anything I cook that is browned more than one degree beyond a pale tan.

It's eight o'clock in the morning, but this is the first food she's craved in two days, so Christine goes to the freezer and gets her a lime Frozfruit. Although I tend to be the one with the strict rules about sweets, this is not dessert so much as revival. Lulu rises to eat, and soon she is slurping happily on her treat.

After making sure she is comfortable, I head to my local office. My work has picked up again, and keeping track of my various clients, student papers, faculty articles, phone messages, and e-mails is a nearly full-time occupation. Nevertheless, in the best tradition of procrastination, I ignore my work to write something on my blog and then read some of the postings.

For several weeks I have been meaning to try a gnocchi recipe one of my readers has sent me. It calls for ricotta cheese, flour, and egg rather than potato, and sounds like just the thing my kids might like, particularly since I know Lulu loves homemade pasta. The reader promises it is easy to make, without the complications or temperamentality of potato gnocchi. I print out the recipe and fold it into my laptop bag, already hungry, my food inertia beginning to thaw.

Then it's back to work, juggling the phone calls and competing obligations like a circus clown, hoping that nothing falls, breaks, or explodes in my face. This is another version of the dream life, but a version in which comedy veers close to tragedy before spiraling into farce. There are only so many hours in the day, and never enough to answer all the calls, reply to the messages, read the papers, conduct the research, draft the memos, maintain the blog, pitch the stories, write the articles, and still have time to coach baseball and softball practice and then get home for dinner. Perhaps there are places in the country where men (and women) have found the right balance, but Westport, Connecticut, is not one of them.

If there is such a mythical land of balance, however—where

parents do not struggle to pay bills, feed the children, and find twenty-two minutes to enjoy a television program—I'm not sure where it's located. One thing that has struck me from reading blog posts for eight months is how many people agonize over the choices they have made. One couple moves to the Midwest for a better job opportunity but misses their East Coast family (especially when the husband's mother gets ill). Another moves to the suburbs, then moves right back to Manhattan. A mother quits her job to stay home with the children, but finds herself lost without the structure of an office. A father plays "Mr. Mom" and endures the questions and stares of other men at cocktail parties.

There are no perfect endings, just war stories. Tales from a front where the enemy is unseen, unwashed, ourselves.

"Who's balancing?" asks a friend. "We're free-falling."

But "balancing," I think, is a good word, as opposed to, say, "balanced." The gerund reflects an ongoing process, a shifting and sorting where different weights are placed on the scales and our lives seesaw back and forth. My best days are those I spend working in town, leaving my office by five, picking up something for dinner, cooking, cleaning, helping with the homework, putting the kids to bed. But then the car needs new tires or the bill for piano lessons comes due, and the seesaw swings upward, leaving me perched and dangling at an impossible height.

I remind myself that the good days are good and the bad days should be limited. This is not always an easy thing to do, because I'm a person who tends to dwell on the negative. The glass is not just half-empty, it's nearly gone, never to be filled again. When I can't find time to write, I will never write another word. When my children don't eat my food, they are wretched savages without hope of redemption. It takes an act of will to focus on the positive, to remember that life is short, our loved ones precious, a bad day at home beats the best day on the road. If I needed proof, I just have to look back eight months. Is everything perfect? No. Is it better than before? Yes. Keep going, keep moving, keep balancing.

Pep talk over, I shut down my computer, forward my phone to voice mail, lock my office, and drive home.

Simon greets me at the door, his face illuminated by the big toothy smile he's inherited from his mother. He wants me to know he scored 100 on his math test. I congratulate him, kissing his sandy hair (which has grown nearly as long as his sister's) and running my hand along the back of his neck. Lulu bounds into the kitchen, obviously in better health. She tells me she watched five hours of television today. I look at Christine, and she shrugs.

"She wasn't feeling well."

"She's made a miraculous recovery."

"And they say TV is bad for you!"

Dinner is pesto, again. Christine has put the water on to boil, but I'm the one who actually drains the pasta and scoops in the pesto from a store-bought container. Salad comes from a bag of mixed greens. The bread is store-bought, heated in the oven by Christine, but removed, sliced, and placed on the table by me. Lulu sets the table, although Christine helps her by bringing out the dishes and glasses. This raises the philosophical question of who has actually "cooked" dinner, which has more than theoretical implications.

"You have to clean the kitchen," says Christine.

"I cooked dinner," I say.

"I cooked dinner," she insists.

"How hard is it to boil water?"

"I bought the pesto, and the bread," she points out. "I was planning on cooking."

"You don't get credit for thinking about cooking."

"I didn't want to clean up. That's why I made dinner."

"But you didn't make it."

And so on, until Christine offers a compromise: If I clean up, she will bathe the children. Given how few pots have been dirtied, I accept the deal. Bathing also means mopping a flooded floor, while cleaning up means listening to music. When Christine leaves, I plug in my iPod and dance around the kitchen, throwing things away, wrapping other things in plastic, and sticking everything else in the dishwasher. Usually it bothers me to find a huge pot taking up half the bottom rack, but now I see the advantage in letting the machine do the work.* I wipe down the table, let Sugar eat the crumbs, and spray Fantastik on the countertops. There is something therapeutic about cleaning a surface, like cutting the lawn or shoveling the driveway, the clear demarcation between work and not-work satisfyingly visible. If only life could be so straightforward, with every effort yielding a measurable result.

I fight the urge to check my e-mail, and instead head upstairs, where the kids are reading in bed.

"Feeling better?" I ask Lulu.

"My stomach hurts," she says, but her grimace is too perfect to be genuine. She's a good actor, this daughter of mine, and has a bright future playing recovering flu patients seeking sympathy from their father, which I give her in double doses.

"Should I pump it?" I ask, pressing down slightly on her abdomen.

"Daddy, stop," she giggles. I stop, and she says, "Do it again!"

I pump her a few more times, until she is laughing so hard I worry she will be sick again. We then turn to more mundane matters like reading, followed by tucking in, and adjusting the door so

---

* According to *Consumer Reports*, it is almost more efficient and economical to place pots in the dishwasher than to clean them by hand. The magazine also recommends that dishes not be rinsed before being placed in the rack, a habit that is hard to shake.

it remains open and casts no scary shadows against the wall. When all is well, I press her brow, give her a kiss, and cross the hall to Simon's room, where he and Christine are reviewing the baseball almanac.

"First father and son to hit back-to-back home runs?" Simon asks.

Christine is stumped.

"Barry and Bobby Bonds?" I guess.

"They never played together," says Simon, with the kind of disdain reserved for the sports-impaired. "Ken Griffey, Jr., and Ken Griffey, Sr."

Balancing also means weighing your children's interests against your own view of their best interests. While some fathers might insist their children memorize multiplication tables and state capitals, others take joy in their children's knowledge of baseball trivia. My own parents discouraged my writing, steering me toward science and medicine out of fear of the alternatives and a sense that I couldn't be trusted to know what I really wanted. As I witness Simon and Lulu developing their own strong preferences, I vow to support them while trying to guide them, keeping my own prejudices at bay. The struggle over food reflects this same dynamic: We can force our children to eat everything we make, imposing our will and fomenting their resentment; or we can accommodate their preferences, creating narcissistic tykes. Or we can strive for a balance between what we know is good for them and what they want to eat.

I kiss my baseball-obsessed son good night and head to my own bedroom. Christine joins me with the page proofs for a book she is editing. I try to read for a while, but either my book is boring or I am very tired. In about fifteen minutes, I am woozy with sleepiness. I look over to tell Christine that I have to turn off the lights, but she is already asleep, the pages scattered over her thighs. Slowly, we become our own parents, I think. This makes me laugh, and if Christine were not asleep, I know she would laugh with me. My own father hasn't seen ten o'clock since 1985. Soon, neither will I.

The next morning I leave early, before anyone is awake. Although I am teaching in New York, I plan to take the 4:07 home, which will give me enough time to shop before I cook. This means leaving Tribeca by 3:30, which is absurdly early for a man with a full-time job. Fortunately, academia accommodates the schedule of a working parent, which may explain why the majority of teachers are women.* On the train, I can read a half-dozen papers and prepare my notes for the next class. By the time I arrive at the Green's Farms station, I have completed another hour of work.

Then it's off to the supermarket, where the dairy aisles are colder than Alaska in April. If this is supposed to be an inducement to shopping, the store managers need to go back to Marketing 101. I grab a carton of eggs and a tub of ricotta cheese and hightail it out of there for the warmer climes of the register line. I choose self-service, scanning the bar codes on my few items and paying by ATM card. We've come a long way since (the first) President Bush was flummoxed by bar codes in a supermarket, and it's only a matter of time until everything has a radio frequency tag and we can literally walk out of the supermarket with our groceries the way we drive through a toll booth with an E-ZPass. The latest technology, however, can never replace the home-cooked meal. No amount of flash-freezing, microwave heating, chemical bonding, or transfaterization will improve on the taste of a meal prepared by hand, in which each ingredient is identifiable and pronounceable without a science text. Or so we can hope.

---

*According to the U.S. Census Bureau, women comprise 79% of elementary and middle school teachers, 59% of secondary teachers, and 46% of postsecondary teachers, for a total percentage of 71% of all teachers.

I find the house empty but unlocked upon my return. A note from Christine says she's taken the dog and the kids for a walk. In the kitchen I measure out the flour and beat the eggs in a bowl. Then I scoop out two cups of ricotta cheese and fold it into the flour. There's something about ricotta cheese that is slightly repellent. Perhaps it's the squishy consistency, or the bland, faintly milky taste. Or maybe it's just that it comes in a big plastic container like yogurt, something no cheese ought to do. It can't be sliced or grated, and few people would ever spread it on a cracker like Boursin or Brie. I must accept on faith that it is the key ingredient in the gnocchi, and that my children will be unaware of its presence.

I mix the three ingredients, adding a little more flour to get a spongy, but not sticky, consistency. The doorbell rings multiple times, and there's Lulu with leopard print tights and her hair pulled back in pigtails. I can't open the door with my hands slippery with dough, but by the time I wash them off in the sink, she has burst inside.

"Daddy, Sugar ate a rabbit!" she says.

"A rabbit?" I asked, incredulous.

"She tried to. She had it in her mouth, but she dropped it."

Christine and Simon are inside now, and Christine explains that Sugar got loose and chased down a rabbit. By the time Christine caught her, she was shaking the rabbit in her mouth.

"I don't think she wanted to eat it," says Christine. "She just wanted to play."

"We could've had rabbit stew," I say.

"Yuck," says Christine.

Our neighbor has a cat who brings home birds; maybe our dog will start bringing home rabbits. Now if only we could teach her to cook.

Lulu wants to know what I am making, and when I tell her,

she asks if she can help. This is an unexpected offer, and one I am thrilled to accept. I explain that each dumpling needs an indentation in the center to help hold its shape, and that her pinky is the perfect size for doing it. We grab a stool so Lulu can reach the table, and she eagerly dabs her fingers into some loose flour to prepare them for the task ahead.

After a couple more kneads, the dough is ready. I roll it into cigar-shaped lengths on the countertop, then cut each length into one-inch pieces. Lulu sprinkles them with some additional flour, and I show her how to press her finger gently into the center. Pretty soon we have an efficient little organization: me rolling and cutting, Lulu dusting and poking. She's actually quite helpful, and the individual gnocchi begin to pile up on a platter. It's difficult to believe we will actually be able to cook and eat these doughy lumps, but I reserve judgment while we sift, shake, and poke.

There's a lot of dough, and rolling it all takes a while, but Lulu never tires. She's quicker than I am, and she tells me to hurry up when I fall behind. Christine hears her and laughs. "She's your daughter," she says.

My daughter, yes, but she also has her mother's cheekbones, her love of words, and an irrepressible sensibility that often finds them both rolling on the floor jiggling with laughter. Someday, not too long from now, the two of them will make a formidable comedy routine, a mother-daughter slapstick team. Right now, however, she's covered with flour in the kitchen.

Finally, we finish forming the gnocchi. Lulu wants to add them to the boiling water. Although this seems slightly dangerous, she's certainly earned it. I hold her elbow while she slides the platter of gnocchi into the pot. The steam swirls up ominously around her hand, but she carefully keeps her distance, and in a few seconds the gnocchi have all safely sunk to the bottom.

We wash up and wipe down, and Lulu even sets the table. I

chop some red cabbage, iceberg lettuce, carrots, and cucumbers for the salad—crunchy things that I know Simon and Lulu like. Sourdough rolls are warming in the toaster oven, and a tomato sauce bubbles on the stove. The kitchen buzzes and hops with activity as the dog sniffs about for crumbs and Simon and Christine are drawn by the smell of dinner. Simon flips a tennis ball against a wall and it ricochets into the cabinets, causing Sugar to scramble to retrieve it.

"Balls outside," says Christine.

"Aw, mom," says Simon, as if he can't believe the kitchen isn't a perfectly reasonable place to play tennis.

By now the gnocchi are floating at the top of the boiling water, a sure sign they are cooked. I empty the water through a strainer, slide the gnocchi into a favorite bowl, add the sauce, and serve.

We sit down together at our modest table as if we lived in Italy or Spain, some European country where people don't wolf down their meals, where conversation is valued, where food is home-cooked, homemade, simple, and good. Where the generations can come together across a table, and dinner is the bridge that connects them. Here we are all immigrants, wandering in search of our promised land. Yet perhaps it is closer than we imagine, right here on our plates, moisturous, luscious, tender, and warm.

And the gnocchi? Simon has thirds, and Lulu—she has seconds.

A Father's Day

In a big country, as the song goes, dreams stay with you. We move, we commute, we are restless and unmoored, but thoughts of home keep us tethered and secured.

Years ago, I promised Christine that New York was an adventure, one we would embark upon together, and if it didn't last, or we tired of it, we could always return to Seattle or Portland, her two first choices, northwestern cities she considered her home. But careers are built, children are born, houses bought, mortgages obtained, friends made, and pretty soon a tree grows in Westport, difficult to transplant, to grow in any other soil. If we ever needed reaffirmation that we are rooted to this place, our flirtation with Kansas City confirmed it. She is not quite a northeasterner, and will never be a Yankee (though a Yankees fan), but Christine has gradually adjusted to a life three thousand miles from the place she was born.

Thus, instead of weekends in the Palouse, we have contented ourselves with yearly visits to the Northwest and the kindness of cousins who, seeking adventure and a foldout sofa, came to New York for the bright lights and big city. But the visits ceased abruptly when we moved to Connecticut, perhaps because Main Street could never compete with Broadway, or maybe because the state seemed as far from the center of the universe as it sometimes felt to us.

So it is with mounting excitement that we count down the days until Christine's cousin Terri and her daughter Maria will visit, our high school graduation gift to Maria, a sparkling seventeen-year-old who has never set foot in Manhattan and whose sense of geography may be just impaired enough to think of a trip to Westport as a visit to the West Village.

"When is Maria coming?" Lulu asks at breakfast.

"Three more days," I say.

"I know that, Dad. I meant *when* is Maria coming?"

Lulu likes precision, mathematical certainty. The more decimal points, the better. I explain that their plane is landing at 5:05 P.M. at LaGuardia, and that I will pick them up. But even that is not precise enough. Finally, we settle on three days, eleven hours, and twenty-five minutes.

"Exactly?" Lulu asks.

"Exactly," I confirm.

In fact, I am not far off. On Saturday night I pull in to the driveway at 7:15 P.M, only twenty minutes later than predicted. Lulu does not seem impressed by the accuracy of my prediction, however; she is too busy escorting Maria about the house to notice. Maria has her father's olive coloring and her mother's pale blue eyes, an unusual and exotic combination. She also has the sweetest disposition a parent could ever hope for, and a bright white smile that rarely seems to waver. I spend the rest of their visit trying to learn whether nature or nurture deserves the credit, and more important, how I can bottle some of her temperament to keep for my own use on special (and traumatic) occasions.

It would be an exaggeration to say Christine is a different person in their presence, but just as when we visited the Northwest, the comfort of familiar faces, recognizable accents, and a common history relaxes her in a way I rarely witness in the Northeast. It makes me realize again how difficult it is to raise a family without the support of relatives, in a place that has no particular hold on us except for a good public school system. Even the fifty miles that separates us from my own parents and brother (and the two hundred miles that separates us from my sister and only nephew) contributes to our feeling of isolation, and to the joy we feel when someone like Maria comes into our home.

On Sunday, Christine takes her cousins to play tourist in New York City while I remain at the house with the kids. She calls me from Chinatown to say they're going to stay for dinner, so I grill some chicken and hot dogs for us. When they arrive home, at nearly eleven o'clock, they are exhausted, worn out, and blistered, but Maria has a grin that can only arise from seeing one of the greatest cities in the world for the very first time. Christine tells me they walked nearly six miles, from Grand Central through SoHo, Tribeca, the World Trade Center site, then on to Chinatown. Yet despite the scope of their tour, they have barely begun to scratch the surface of everything there is to visit, and wish they could have stayed the night.

"You can," I say, realizing suddenly how easy it would be. My parents have a small apartment in Manhattan, and I'm certain they would let Christine stay there with her cousins. I have recovered well enough from the trauma of my first extended experience playing solo parent that I'm pretty confident I could handle it with minimal injury (to the kids or myself). Law school classes have ended, and I can arrange my schedule to work at home for the next few days. All in all, I suggest they seize the opportunity while the seizing is good.

"Are you sure?" Terri asks, like someone who can't believe her luck and doesn't want to spook it.

"Sure, I'm sure," I say.

Christine gets on the Internet while I leave my parents a voice mail message, and pretty soon a plan is in place for two days hence.

I leave for work the next morning before anyone is awake, and when I return, Terri has made spaghetti with meatballs for dinner. It's a dish I've tried to sell several times without success, but with Maria watching, Lulu eats three meatballs and Simon has four. When I ask Terri for her secret, she tells me it's marrying an Italian man. Since this is not an option for me (the man or the Italian), I freeze the remaining meatballs and hope Lulu will remember.

Those of us who did not cook, clean, then those of us not visiting New York the next day do our homework, brush our teeth, and retire to our bedrooms. Christine stays up late with her cousins planning, plotting, and scheming their escape from the suburbs. It's past midnight when she sneaks into bed.

"Thank you, Cameron," she says.

No thanks are needed, I tell her. Being home more often this year has made me realize how difficult Christine's life has been out here in the suburbs, her struggle to transition from city mom to country mom, from walking mom to driving mom, from poet mom to PTA mom, all without her own mother and the rest of her family two plane flights away. It's Christine I should thank, for the years she has had to raise our children with little help, for the efforts she has made to keep our family eating wisely and well, for putting up with my moods, complaints, and absences like a super spouse: Wonder Wife.

It's not until the following afternoon that I regret my largesse. With two kids to care for, my day begins at 6:30 A.M. and doesn't end until 9:00 P.M. From 3:30 until 5:30 P.M. I am in the car continuously, driving from Westport to Fairfield to Norwalk and back again, to gymnastics, a birthday party, and Hebrew school. Simon and Lulu use the time to whack each other on the head, punch each other in the arm, and otherwise inflict pain and torture in creative and productive ways. By the time we arrive at our house, I am beginning to think a Plexiglas partition between passengers is the only solution.

They open their doors and race from the car before I even stop, laughing gleefully (or demonically) while continuing their shenanigans. I jump out after them and yell about the dangers of moving vehicles, small garages, cranky dads.

"Sorry, Daddy," says Simon, pawing at the concrete with one oversized foot.

"Daddy," asks Lulu, "what are we having for dinner?"

It is at that moment my entire world shifts. There is no other way to explain it. As Lulu looks at me, her eyes bright with the anticipation of what I might have planned for dinner, looking forward to it with the same excitement she would muster for a new episode of SpongeBob, my fury deflates completely, replaced by something like revelation. It is more than impossible to be angry; it is inconceivable not to fall immediately in love with her and Simon. I have traveled from the father who was never home for dinner to the father without whom dinner is unimaginable. In my daughter's mind, I am not only present for dinner, I am an essential ingredient. Shake, salt, stir, add Dad. Despite their complaints about browned breadcrumbs or oily artichokes, I realize my efforts this year have not fallen on numb tongues. Each meal is a new journey, a new adventure, and they are happy to come along, even if they don't always applaud my culinary destination.

Of course, I don't have anything planned, but I pull parenting trick 101 from the book and ask her what she wants.* "Fresh pasta!" she says, without missing a beat.

Fortunately, I have the eggs and flour in the house, and in just about thirty minutes—with Lulu working the pasta maker—I have dinner made. Simon specifically requests the tomato sauce I made for the gnocchi: chopped onions, carrots, and celery, with a quarter cup of light cream added to the crushed tomatoes just before serving. It's easy to prepare, and if I dice the onions finely and surreptitiously, my children don't even know they're in there. Two handfuls of iceberg lettuce, leftover red cabbage, and a sliced cucumber, and we have salad. It seems like I should have a bottle of white wine—something French and saucy—but I don't, and in any case I don't like to drink alone. Instead, Simon fills a pitcher with ice water and sets it on the table. Lulu gives everyone silverware and folds a napkin carefully under each fork. I bring the pasta to the table and scoop it onto their plates.

We eat, the three of us, in happy contemplation of the wonder of wheat, chickens, fire. That we are able to put these incongruent things together and produce a meal is, simply, miraculous. The most profound shift in human culture occurred when we learned to cultivate rather than relying on hunting and foraging. I don't claim to have experienced a transformation on a similar scale, but preparing food for my family rather than scavenging at Grand Central Terminal has been its own cultural turning point, a personal watershed of domestic proportions.

I look at my two children and realize how much things have changed, and what a difference a dad can make.

"More pasta," says Simon.

"Me, too," says Lulu.

---

* This is a variant on teacher trick 101: lob the question back at the questioner.

Happier words have rarely been heard. I feel like my old Jewish grandmother, hovering over the *kinderlach,* wishing nothing more than that they *essen, bubeleh, essen.* Despite the clichés and the hoary advice, one can see how food becomes love, and love becomes food, and the more you give of one the more you get of the other. Food creates relevance, meaning, presence. It is a touchstone of parenting, an easy way to measure success: How are they eating? What are they eating? Are they eating enough? And though, as I have learned, their refusal to eat doesn't necessarily mean a failure of parenting, it sure feels good when they gobble it down.

The phone rings. It's Christine. She wants to let us know her cousins are having a fantastic time, and to check if we are surviving.

"We're great," I say, and we are. A year ago I would not have been here—either literally or metaphorically. Now, I honestly welcome the opportunity to have Simon and Lulu to myself, to cook for them, help them with their homework, get them ready for bed. These tasks require a completely different set of skills from making money, writing, lecturing students about libel and privacy, but just as lifting weights exercises different muscle groups than running nine miles, the combination feels essential and necessary for balance, fitness, health.

"Daddy made pasta," Lulu says to the telephone.

I can hear Christine telling Lulu she's lucky to have such a yummy dinner, to which Lulu responds, her voice plaintive and pleading, "When will you be home, Mommy?"

This, too, is the joy of parenting: Victories are short-lived; triumphs are measured in inches; today's favorite parent is tomorrow's forgotten goat. But I don't take it too hard, especially when both Simon and Lulu fight to have me read them a book, sit on their bed, tuck them in last.

When the lights are out and the house is dark, I walk around downstairs in a kind of Zen calm. If I were a more religious person, I might say a blessing, or burn an offering. Instead, I say my own prayers, thank a god for the life I have, the health of my family, the good fortune I've shared, and the bountiful food I can purchase at Stop & Shop. Then I knock on wood, as my grandmother might have done. She was a woman who knew from hard luck and tough choices, yet she never stopped cooking, perhaps because the pleasure she received from filling her children's and grandchildren's plates kept despair at a safe distance.

On Friday, when Christine returns with her cousins, they are practically shimmering with overstimulation. Manhattan is a dream, and Maria was the dreamer. Even Christine sighs, "I love New York," in the same tone as someone might say, "I love Brad Pitt," or "I love Givenchy couture"—equally unobtainable, yet representing some perfect ideal, some platonic state that no doubt would prove disappointing if ever actually possessed, but well worth the fantasy.

Because I have been on dinner duty the last three nights, Terri and Christine take over, frying chicken and baking lasagna. The weekend weather is spectacular, harbinger of summer, and we rush from baseball diamond to softball field and back again. Simon smacks a triple and two singles, while Lulu connects on the first pitch to knock the ball out of the infield. Already, both of my children have surpassed my athletic ability, which is every father's fondest wish. I'd like to claim it's my genetic legacy, but given my father's myopia, my mother's flat feet, and my own upper body weakness, it's somebody's genes, but not my own. Nor can I attribute it to the solid diet of meat and potatoes, hearty breakfasts, and thick ham sandwiches. The only explanation is good air and lots of sleep.

"You have great kids," says Terri. Coming from a woman

whose own children were the best behaved teenagers I have ever seen, that's no small compliment. I know she means to praise our parenting skills, but I also hear it as an admonition: *Don't forget how great your family is; don't take them for granted; don't lose your temper when you should be calm; don't cry when you can laugh. Most of all, be grateful.*

"Thank you," I say.

Because it's Saturday night, we make popcorn and stay up late watching a movie. Maria has Christine's laptop, and she surfs the Internet and IMs her friends. When her mother asks what she's doing, she answers, "Nothing." I'm happy to see that despite her perfect smile, she is still at heart a teenager. Lulu nods off against her shoulder, but pretends she's still awake when I try to take her upstairs. Maria doesn't mind; she leans into Lulu like an older sister, happy to have her baby sis on her arm. Simon and I debate the merits of the movie's finale, and Lulu wakes up just long enough to resist brushing her teeth. When we get upstairs, we crowd into Lulu's bed with Sugar, and Simon and Lulu decide to have a sleepover. As someone who can barely sleep in a king-sized bed with his own wife, it never ceases to amaze me how children can crowd two or three in a single bed and fall instantly asleep, but they can, and they do. Christine goes back downstairs to chat with her cousins, and I soon join Simon and Lulu in Neverland.

I wake on Sunday to a kitchen smelling of pancakes and coffee. It's Father's Day, and my children surprise me by waking before I do and decorating the kitchen with streamers and colored paper. Lulu bounces into my lap, and Simon gives me a hug. "Happy Father's Day," he says.

"I thought every day was Father's Day," I say.

"No, every day is kids' day," says Lulu. "Except Father's Day."

"And Mother's Day," adds Simon.

"So you get 363 days and we only get two?" I ask.

"Yup," says Simon.

"Hmm. Doesn't sound fair to me." But I accept a cup of coffee from Christine, and the newspaper from Simon, and soon forget the mathematical inequities.

In my gift boxes there are DVDs, fancy shaving cream and soap, a tie imprinted with golden retrievers ("Sugar picked it out," says Lulu), boxer shorts that proclaim me "World's Best Dad," and two cookbooks. Though I don't feel deserving of the title (the competition is stiff; so many other outstanding performances; I'd like to thank my manager and agent . . .), I do feel extremely lucky.

"What do you want to do today?" Christine asks.

"Make dinner?" I ask.

"It's Father's Day," says Christine.

But I'm serious. It's Terri and Maria's last day on the East Coast, and a big meal seems an appropriate send-off. If it's not clear to everyone by now, I enjoy cooking—don't think of it as a chore, prefer to eat my own food, find joy in putting it on the table, would rather not clean up.

"Okay," says Christine. "It's your day."

Thus, it is decided: black bean burritos.

I spend the rest of the morning on my throne in the family room while servants feed me grapes and tend to my every need. Or maybe that's a dream. In reality, I am corralled into hanging some pictures Christine has been meaning to put up for months, cleaning broken branches that have fallen on the driveway, and repairing a screen door Simon has kicked too hard. I do get to go for a run, and Christine makes me a second pot of coffee. Later in the day I read the entire Sunday paper, including the advertising inserts. When it's time to cook, Terri helps chop peppers and onions and makes the guacamole. Lulu sets the table with Maria's assistance. Simon fills glasses with water, and Christine opens a bottle of wine.

It feels like a last supper. Tomorrow, Christine's family returns home. In about a week, school ends, and with it, Dinner with Dad. I try not to think about endings while I make Simon a second burrito, but an air of melancholy hangs heavy over the table. Lulu insists that Maria stay, and when Maria says she has to get home to start a job, Lulu bursts into tears. We promise her that Maria will return, but it's been a long day, Lulu is tired, and it takes the rest of the evening to console her and get everyone into bed and ready for school the next morning.

When the kids are finally asleep, Christine helps her cousins pack in the downstairs bedroom. I sit at the kitchen table with my Father's Day cards arrayed like Boy Scout tents, two by two in neat little rows.

I pick up Lulu's card. On the cover, she has drawn a strikingly accurate portrait of herself and me. She is skinny and tall, with bright yellow hair and big blue eyes. I am skinny and taller, with no hair and blue eyes. She holds my hand, her stick fingers intertwined with mine. Our mouths are curved into wide open smiles, as if we were singing a song together, something upbeat and lively, like Lulu herself.

I open the card. Inside she has written: "I love my Dad because he takes care of me when I am hurt."

I set the card down on the table. I feel my breath catch in my throat. For a moment I stare out the window into the darkness of the backyard. I can hear Christine's voice rise and fall, her cousins responding. I think that it wasn't that long ago I was sitting at this same table, looking out this same window. But then I saw gloom; now I see a glimmer. Then I saw the beginning of another day, long before it should begin, the ending nowhere in sight. Now I see the comfort of home, the warmth of my family and friends, faith, hope, joy.

"Cameron?" Christine calls.

"I'm here," I say. Then I rise from the table and join her in the other room.

Dinner with Dad

Over the course of nearly ten months, I sat down to dinner with my family 231 times, averaging 5.5 meals per week and missing my self-imposed quota of sharing at least 5 meals a week only twice. I cooked dinner a total of 80 times, making 35 different meals and (not counting vacation weeks) averaging 2.05 meals per week, which was slightly under my goal of 2.5 times per week. The meals included black bean burritos, black bean fajitas, pizza, hamburgers and hot dogs, steak, fresh pasta with tomato sauce, pasta with pesto, penne with tomato sauce (with artichokes and without), spaghetti with Bolognese sauce, pasta with smothered onions, gnocchi (store-bought and homemade), fried chicken (with beer batter and without), Israeli couscous, shrimp with pasta (and with edamame and couscous), egg rolls and Chinese noodles, tofu stir-fry, fried rice, spicy peanut noodles, lasagna, falafel, scrod with baked stuffed potatoes, pasties, risotto, ziti, spaghetti with vegetarian meatballs, white chili, tofu loaf with mashed potatoes, saffron orzo, cassoulet, macaroni and cheese, raclette, grilled chicken, and breakfast for dinner.

Measured by how many of these meals my children actually enjoyed, my efforts were a failure. But measured by how many new foods my children were encouraged to try, and how broadly they expanded their tastes, my cooking was a success. To her repertoire of plain pasta and chicken nuggets, Lulu added burritos, hamburgers, homemade pasta, homemade pizza, gnocchi, ziti, fried chicken (sometimes), and Terri's meatballs. Simon was more adventurous, and came to love shrimp, small amounts of tomato sauce (on homemade pasta), risotto, couscous, falafel, egg rolls, and Chinese noodles, in addition to all the foods Lulu enjoyed. In all, they at least tripled the number of different foods they were willing to eat. As for Christine, she gained eight pounds in ten months.

Measured by how many meals we shared, and how much time we spent together at the table, the year was an even more significant achievement. In August, I was lucky if I had dinner with my family once or twice a week. By June, my children expected me home for dinner, and my wife planned around it. I was able to help Simon with his math homework and teach Lulu to tie her shoes. I had time to coach their sports teams and play "Is it true?" at the dinner table. We all taught a puppy how to be a dog, and learned to care for another animal that needed love. We cleared, cleaned, and washed up together, our hands in the sink, our hands on each other.

Getting home for dinner wasn't easy; but it wasn't all that difficult, either. I found it just required the commitment and wherewithal to say "No, thanks" to the late phone call, the garrulous client, the lingering student, my own laziness. As I have noted, it was not unlike training for a race, with its good days and bad days. I just had to do it. Of course, *just doing it* is often easier said than done, as anyone who has tried to go on a diet or train for a marathon knows. What seems so simple in theory can prove quite difficult in practice. Clients don't always take no for an answer, and sometimes I didn't really want them to.

More difficult than getting home, however, was finding time to cook 2.5 meals a week. It seems like it shouldn't be hard, but it is. Very hard. For one thing, deciding on a menu and then shopping and prepping for it before the kids starve (or melt down) is nearly impossible for a working parent, and probably impossible for a single parent. This explains the success of "thirty-minute meals" and meal assembly centers. When you're getting home at 5:30 or 6:00, you better have something in the freezer or you're eating takeout. And another thing: If you lack the organizational skills of a neurosurgeon or the culinary wizardry of a celebrity chef, you will soon find yourself cooking the same meals over and over again. I have a great deal of sympathy for parents who get stuck in a rut, making the same three or four dinners a week. Coming up with original meals was often exhausting, and without reward. Of the thirty-five different meals I made for dinner, Lulu embraced just six or seven, which is scant incentive to keep creating new ones.

In the end, my failure to make my 2.5-meal goal was partly a reflection of this difficulty in getting my children to try something new. There were times when I probably should have cooked, and instead I chose to reheat something in the microwave or take the kids to the diner. Fighting over artichokes just didn't seem worth it. As much as I like to experiment, I take rejection very badly.* Especially toward the end of the year, when I felt as if I'd made

---

*Not a great trait for a writer, which is probably another reason I continue to practice law.

everything I could possibly get my kids to eat, my desire to cook something new and different waned precipitously.

But my failure to make dinner 2.5 times a week was also a reflection of my wife's emergence as an equal partner in the dinner experiment, rediscovering her desire to cook and taking the pressure off me. In fact, there were nights when I planned to cook, only to learn Christine had already prepared something. Between the two of us, we had something hot and homemade on the table at least six nights a week, including nights when I wasn't home.

The biggest hurdle I had to overcome during the year was my own desire to win a prize for cooking—to make the fanciest, most complicated recipe I could find—as if my own kids would be so wowed with my prowess in the kitchen that they would feel compelled to eat whatever I cooked. Because my personal operating manual required that I not only undertake the most challenging tasks, but also demand a trophy for my success, learning to disregard my own ego was problematic at best. At times, it was my worst enemy, as I let my children pull my strings and behaved worse than a child myself. I've had to learn, and relearn, that children don't give prizes; they expect them. It is the wise adult who knows (and remembers) the difference.

The most important thing I've come to understand in this year of eating dangerously, this year of dining with Dad, is that we can't change our lives by insisting other people accommodate us. When I yelled at Lulu for refusing to eat artichokes, it didn't make her want to eat them; just the opposite. When I fought with my wife about working at home, it didn't make her want to have me around; just the opposite. The most successful meals were the ones where my children participated in choosing the menu, prepping the ingredients, cooking the food. This is not always an easy thing to do—it requires patience, compromise, a strong stomach—but it works. Like life, the messy parts are often the most rewarding, but you have to get dirty first.

Of course, not everything is perfect. As I write this, I still grapple with the financial consequences of my decision to get home for dinner. It's not clear to me whether we will remain in Westport, with its great schools and expensive housing, or move farther north (increasing my commute), or leave the state entirely—although I'm pretty certain there are no jobs for First Amendment litigators in the Palouse. And as Christine has let me know, *too much togetherness* has made her appreciate me less. We continue to struggle to find the right balance between absence and oppression, and I continue to wonder whether I'm immature or just a baby. Even though my children have enjoyed having me home, I still have to learn to tame my emotions, to accept rejection, and to handle chaos and uncertainty. To be, in other words, a better parent.

As I try to sort it all out, searching for the big conclusion that will explain the origin of the universe, the nature of time, and the meaning of life, my children grow, evolve, and constantly astound me. One morning, not long after I make my final meal, Christine comes into my office and asks if I will take Lulu down the street to a playdate.

It's a beautiful day, hot and languid, a great day to be a kid, or have a kid, or just feel like a kid. I shut off my computer, grab my shoes, and put a leash on the dog. I call upstairs for Lulu, and she comes downstairs in a pair of shorts, a T-shirt, and sandals. Sugar greets her with a furry snuffle, and I get a kiss as well.

"Ready?" I ask.

She nods, her ponytail bopping like jubilance.

We walk out the front door, onto the green of our front lawn, maple trees casting a luxurious shade along the border of the road. Lulu turns to me and says, "Dad, it's great to live on the same street with your best friend and be able to walk there every day."

I realize that these are the moments to cherish, holding your daughter's hand as you stroll across the grass to her best friend's house. Not to forget them, never to forget them, no matter how tired you may be at the end of the day, or what frustrations you might have to deal with, or what tragedies (God forbid) you may have to face. That's the point, isn't it, of dining with Dad, or of dining with anyone: to live in the moment as if it were the last.

Peace.

Acknowledgments

This is a work of nonfiction. Some names have been changed, but no composite meals were created. I tried to keep an accurate record of our dinners and our conversations, but sometimes I forgot to write things down and had to reconstruct them from memory. Other times, I just forced certain things out of my mind, only to recall them painfully, usually late at night. When possible, I put them back in, but tried to make myself look as good as possible.

I could never have begun this book if not for the support of and brilliant advice from my agent at ICM, Lisa Bankoff. She has been my best reader for more than a decade, and I am incredibly fortunate to be able to call her agent, and friend. Her assistant, Tina Dubois Wexler, handles the details with aplomb, and for that I am grateful. I couldn't have kept writing but for the help I received from my able research assistants Caitlin Parker, Isabel Tewes, Nanette Green, and Laurie Moffat. My editor at Random House, Bruce Tracy, straddled the perfect line between nudging and encouraging. His advice was always dead-on, and he was happy to listen to excuses, second thoughts, and complete reversals of strongly held opinions. I also owe a debt to Sally Marvin, Avideh Bashirrad, London King, Karen Fink, Rachel Bernstein, Beth Pearson, and Emily DeHuff at Random House, and to David, Danny, Andrew, and everyone at Hybrid Films, for their efforts on my behalf. Thanks.

Thanks, as well, to the readers and posters on my blog through the year who inspired me, in particular: cks, chachlilmum (for her great gnocchi recipe), Audrey, Susan, and Richie H (for the Bad Dad test). Their words of wisdom and encouragement kept me cooking when I thought I wouldn't make it. I also owe plenty to my old friend Curt Mark, who taught me some great tricks about writing and cooking. Howard Gordon and Eric Parker don't cook much, but over the years they've listened plenty, and that's made all the difference.

Finally, none of this book could have been written without the willing participation and cooperation of my family—my wife, Christine, and our children, Simon and Lulu. This year was a journey for all of us, and I only hope that one day, many years from now, they forgive me my baked scrod.

About the Author

CAMERON STRACHER is the author of *Double Billing: A Young Lawyer's Tale of Greed, Sex, Lies, and the Pursuit of a Swivel Chair* and a novel, *The Laws of Return.* He is a graduate of Harvard Law School and the Iowa Writers' Workshop. His essays and articles on family life (and other topics) have appeared in *The New York Times, The New York Times Magazine, The Wall Street Journal, Parents, The American Lawyer* (where he is a contributing editor), and many other publications. During the day he teaches at New York Law School and practices media law, and at night he rushes home to his wife and two children in Westport, Connecticut. Visit his website at www.dinnerwithdad.com.

About the Type

This book was set in Caslon, a typeface first designed in 1722 by William Caslon. Its widespread use by most English printers in the early eighteenth century soon supplanted the Dutch typefaces that had formerly prevailed. The roman is considered a "workhorse" typeface due to its pleasant, open apperance, while the italic is exceedingly decorative.

BRADNER LIBRARY
SCHINOLCRAFT COLLEGE
18600 HAGGERTY ROAD
LIVONIA, MICHIGAN 48152

BRADNER LIBRARY
SCHOOLCRAFT COLLEGE
18600 HAGGERTY ROAD
LIVONIA, MICHIGAN 48152